SINJINLANDS

SINJINLANDS

By

Gerard J. St. John

Copyright © 2011 by Gerard J. St. John

All rights reserved. No part of this book may be reproduced, scanned, or distributed in any printed or electronic form without permission.

First Edition: December, 2011
Printed in the United States of America

ISBN: 978-1-105-55993-8

Front Cover Photographs:
Left: Cpl. John St. John, USMCR, Quantico, VA, 1933
Right: 1st Lt. Gerard J. St. John, USMCR, South China Sea, 1962

Table of Contents

Table of Contents 5
Foreword i
I. FRIENDS & FAMILY 1
   THE EYE OF THE CLOCK 3
   THE MORE SHE CRIES 7
   BOCK'S POCONO TRAIL LODGE 15
   AGNES, A Remembrance 23
   A COMMON ENEMY 27
   THE KAISER ON THE CORNER 87
   A TOAST TO TOM WILSON 95
   THE AMBASSADOR FOR SOCCER 99
   THE SMALL CASE LAWYER 101
II. PHILADELPHIA LAWYERS 109
   PRINCE ALBERT 111
   GEORGE THE THIRD 119
   A MORAL ISSUE 125
   FRANK B. MURDOCH: 133
   BARNEY SMOLENS: 143
III. PHILADELPHIA BAR HISTORY 149
   A Forgotten Father 151
   A Man of Letters 159
   WHEN YOU CALL ME THAT, SMILE! 165

 The Giant of the Philadelphia Bar 171
 This is *OUR* Bar!.. 183
IV. FICTION 225
 A SENIOR WEEK STORY 227
Epilogue 259

Foreword

"Sinjin" is how the English pronounce the name "St. John." I learned that from the Jesuits who taught me at St. Joseph's College in Philadelphia. The Jesuits liked that obscure phonetic fact. I like it too. We are not alone.

When I identify myself online as Sinjin, invariably I am told that the name has already been taken by someone else. Some Sinjins are familiar. St. John ("Sinjin") Terrell is well-known in the Philadelphia area as the person who ran the Lambertville Music Circus. Also, he inaugurated the traditional reenactment of Washington crossing the Delaware River on Christmas Eve. Sinjin Smith is a noted beach volleyball player in California. Neither of those Sinjins is related to me.

No one has exclusive rights to the Sinjin name. However, I have a vested interest of about seventy-five years as a Sinjin. Accordingly, I have no qualms about calling this collection of my writings "Sinjinlands."

This compilation includes stories about my family — not just the Sinjins, but also the Metzingers, O'Keefes, Crowleys, Gushues, McIntyres and Schollars who fit under the heading of forebears. Also, there are articles about lawyers, some of whom were like family. I tried to capture their personalities. Other articles are about some of the historical icons of the Philadelphia bar.

Finally, I tried my hand at a work of fiction loosely based on one of the cases that I handled years ago. Some readers may recognize the background setting. I hope that they will realize that the names and statements of the characters in the story are strictly the products of my imagination.

When I published *The War Within* a few months ago, I was surprised to find that it did not display the name of the publisher. When I buy copies from the publisher, the name on the sales slip is Lulu Enterprises, Inc. They have a site on the Internet at Lulu.com. Also absent are an ISBN number and the bar code that usually accompanies it. ISBN means "International Standard Book Number." It is used primarily by libraries, collectors and publishers to identify books and their revisions. An ISBN number also makes it possible to buy books through a variety of sellers, such as amazon.com. I have now decided to add ISBN numbers to both books.

Typically, memoirs have interest only to a small segment of readers who have some connection with the author or the subject matter of the stories. I suspect that the interest in the stories published here will be even more limited. Not many people will be interested in the life of my letter-carrier father. Dad was not the Great Santini. Also, with one possible exception, these stories do not emphasize the weaknesses of the subjects. That one exception is my remembrance of Al Sheppard; but it is hard to celebrate Al's tenacity in overcoming addiction without mentioning addiction.

So there you have it. I will not be surprised if I do not receive any e-mail messages from readers telling me that these stories precipitate a lot of memories. I do not expect that from this book. This book is for me.

gjs

I. FRIENDS & FAMILY

Did you ever sit at an office window, watching automobile traffic swirl through a network of city streets? Each car is operated by a different driver; and each driver is unique. Some drivers are smart; some are less so. Some are better drivers than others. Each car had its own point of origin; and each has a different destination. Yet thousands of cars sweep along as if dancing to a silent symphony, making stops and starts, and turns and pirouettes at the independent direction of thousands of unrelated drivers following only the general rules of a motor vehicle law.

It is like watching clouds change shape as they move through the sky subtly nudged by air currents and pressure changes.

In the course of human events, it sometimes seems that our destinies are subtly directed by forces of heredity and environment. The stories in this chapter describe some of the heredity and environmental influences that I sometimes see when looking back over the past.

THE EYE OF THE CLOCK

It is a part of every game. At some point you become aware of the clock. Your allotted time is running out. Time must be used wisely. If you are ahead of the game, avoid mistakes; take no risks. If you are behind, squeeze every breath out of every remaining second; take calculated risks. He who controls the clock controls the game.

Author Pat Conroy, in his autobiographical book *My Losing Season*, reminisces about his college days, thirty years and eighty pounds ago, when he was a member of the basketball team at The Citadel in Charleston, South Carolina. Conroy's recollection of past events "lit up with consequence" led him inexorably to the conclusion that life can come to an abrupt halt at any moment and that past experiences should be valued. In Conroy's words, "time is a finger snap and an eye blink and . . . you should not allow a moment to pass you by without taking joyous, ecstatic note of it, not wasting a single moment of its swift, breakneck circuit."

But time is more than just a swiftly passing moment. Christopher Nolan titled his autobiography *Under the Eye of the Clock*. Nolan is a tormented man. He was born with cerebral palsy, which produced constant spasms, rendering him unable to use his arms and legs and unable to speak coherently. Those who saw his spastic attempts to move or heard his incoherent attempts to speak quickly concluded that Christopher was an imbecile. They were wrong. As of the time of this writing, he has published three works, a collection of poems, an autobiography and a fictional novel. Reviewers compare him to the Irish writer James Joyce. Nolan does not explain the meaning of the title, *Under the Eye of the Clock*, but an introductory poem suggests that it refers to the chimes of a clock that would wake him from his nostalgic reverie and bring him back to reality. For Nolan, time is the cold reality of the present.

Frank Lammer heard the ticking of a different clock that morning in 1964 when I walked into his office. Frank was the Executive Director of the Redevelopment Authority of the City of Philadelphia, which at that time was the country's showcase of urban renewal. Frank was a short, stocky man, about 57 years of age, with a broad face and black hair combed straight back. He had spent his working life in the real estate business – and the real estate business was booming in Philadelphia during the years when John F. Kennedy's presidency was coupled with the political influence of Congressman Bill Green. Lammer had also been on the adjunct faculty of St. Joseph's College, teaching real estate. He was a past president of the College's Alumni Association and, back in his college days, a member of the track team. The St. Joe connection gave us a common bond. But on this particular morning, something was wrong.

Frank had been in the hospital earlier that week. His face was tense. He seemed to be experiencing discomfort. Looking up from the papers in front of him he blurted, "Every day, things get a little bit worse. No one tells you this but after you reach age 35, your body starts to decline. From that time on, life is downhill; you die a little bit each day. I am 57 years old and things will only get worse." Such pessimism was not like Frank. Usually, he was the type who put his troubles behind him. That is what he did when St. Joe's decided to assign his real estate course to a full-time faculty member, one who had no practical experience in real estate. Frank had created the course. He did not want to give it up. But, Frank sought out that new teacher and gave him all of the notes and teaching plans that he had created over the years. And then Frank put the experience behind him and continued to be an active member of the alumni. But on this day, he must have received a particularly bad medical report. "This probably doesn't mean much to you. You are what, about 30-years old? But when you get past 35 it will mean something." I edged toward the door, searching for a graceful way to get out of that office.

Frank Lammer died several years later. On occasion, I recall that unpleasant conversation, and wonder whether there was any merit to Frank's lament. By the time I passed age 57 without incident, I put the conversation out of my mind. But few years back, the mental picture of Frank Lammer came back when I sat in the office of an obviously fatigued specialist who was looking over the results of my blood work. His medical group was experiencing organizational problems and one result of those problems was that a very busy physician found himself with additional patients to treat but no additional time. He was tired. The results of the preliminary blood test showed the need for a biopsy before he could make a definitive determination whether surgery would be needed. As he scanned the medical file, his fatigued mind added ten years to my age. He then began what must be a routine explanation under the circumstances he perceived. "At age 74, we have to balance the benefit of an invasive diagnostic procedure in light of a life expectancy of about ten years." I quickly pointed out that my age at the time was 64 years, not 74. The biopsy was scheduled and the result was favorable. Surgery was not needed.

That was more than ten years ago. I am now 75 years of age. I wonder if my present age still brings into play the same decision-making criteria cited by that specialist ten years ago? It is *déjà vu*. It is Frank Lammer all over again. Listen! Do you hear it, a faint ticking sound?

"Ah, take the cash, and let the credit go; nor heed the rumble of a distant drum!"

THE MORE SHE CRIES

Movies of recent vintage seem to place a premium on the production of tears. *"Something for Joey"* was inspired by John Cappelletti's tearful dedication of his Heisman Trophy to his younger brother Joey who suffered from terminal cancer. The movie produced at least as many tears as did Cappelletti's emotional dedication, which was broadcast on prime time television. *"Terms of Endearment"* was another lachrymose film. And then there is *"Saving Private Ryan"*, a movie with virtually no plot and a thin story line apparently designed to demonstrate that World War II was fought with real bullets.

The advance billing for *Private Ryan* focused on the preparation of the actors for the combat scenes and how veteran actor Tom Hanks took charge of that preparation and challenged the junior actors to endure the preparation hardships until they "knew what it was like to be Marines." (Apparently, no one told Hanks that Marines were not involved in the invasion of Normandy.) The main focus of television commercials for the film showed clips of elderly war veterans, their eyes weepy and watery after having watched a preview of *"Private Ryan."* It was sad to see those frail old men with their flimsy khaki or blue garrison caps -- the ones that we used to call "piss cutters" -- their hands shaking, voices halting and tears running down their cheeks, trying to express their thoughts about those terrible times gone by.

I wonder how Liz O'Keefe would have reacted to those teary promotions. Liz was no stranger to hardship. She was one tough lady. Elizabeth O'Keefe was born in 1878 in a place that God forgot, Conception Harbour, Newfoundland. She was my grandmother.

Liz St. John, 1948

Conception Harbour is a tiny fishing village located near the closed end of Conception Bay in the southeast corner of the cold triangle of granite that juts out of the North Atlantic at the mouth of the Gulf of St. Lawrence. Conception Harbour was an equal opportunity place. Both the rich and the poor alike worked hard just to stay alive. It was all that those rugged fishermen could do to eke out a subsistence living. Women shared the same hardships and the same dangers as the men.

Liz had a slender build and an erect bearing that gave her the appearance of being taller than her actual height. She was a hard worker, one of those people who is always moving, always doing something. She worked in the home. By the age of seven years, Liz baked loaves of bread. She worked on the docks, repairing nets and drying the catch. And she even worked aboard the fishing ships on occasion, cooking and doing whatever else needed to be done. She was in her early twenties when the chance came to join her brothers in their new-found land of milk and honey, Camden, New Jersey. She never looked back. One morning, Liz O'Keefe and her mother walked out the front door, locked it behind them; and walked away. She would later say, "I t'anked God the day I left that place and I ain't never going back!"

It was in Camden that Liz discovered that Newfoundlanders' English was different from the English that was spoken in the rest of the world. It was not just the way that they pronounced "Newfoundland," with an emphasis on the last syllable. The basic speech variation ran deeper than that. Newfoundland's fishing villages were isolated communities. The country is so far out into the Atlantic that it is in a different time zone, one hour and 30 minutes ahead of Eastern Standard Time. Accessible only by ship in that era, the lack of fertile farm land and the bitter cold weather combined to discourage visitors. Prior to the 1900s, Newfoundlanders had precious little contact with the outside world. As a result, their language patterns and word usage stayed pretty much the same from one generation to the next. In nineteenth century Newfoundland, many communities spoke English almost exactly as it had been spoken three hundred years earlier in the southwest of England. "I's talkin' the way I always talks," Liz would say when asked about her manner of speech.

Fortunately for Liz, Camden, New Jersey was home to many other former Newfoundlanders who spoke substantially the same way. One of them was a bushy-haired young man named Charlie St. John. Charlie was from Avondale, another small Newfoundland fishing village next door to Conception Harbour. Charlie and his brothers and sisters left Newfoundland looking for a better way of life. They were fed up with the constant danger of the north Atlantic, the malnutrition and disease associated with a diet that was lacking in many essential vitamins. And, of course, there was the constant discomfort and the damp cold weather.

Anything had to be better. Most of Charlie's family boarded the ferry south to Nova Scotia, where another ferry took them to Portland, Maine. From there, they worked their way farther south. Agnes, Alice, Maude and Pearl settled in the Boston area. Greg stopped in Camden, New Jersey. Only Jack went back to Avondale.

Charlie was different. He took the Canadian Pacific Railway west across Canada to British Columbia; and then went south to Spokane, Washington. But the wild west of the late 1800s was not for Charlie. He decided to go east to the Philadelphia area where many other Newfoundlanders had found work in the iron construction industry, working on railroads, bridges and modern steel-supported buildings. In Camden, he met Liz O'Keefe. In 1902, Charlie and Liz were married in Nativity B.V.M. Church at Belgrade Street and Allegheny Avenue in the Port Richmond neighborhood of Philadelphia.

Life was no bed of roses for an iron worker's family in turn-of-the-century Philadelphia but, by comparison to life in the old fishing villages, it was not bad at all. Charlie and Liz could not afford to buy a home. They rented houses in Nativity parish, first on Chatham Street, later on Cedar Street and then back to Chatham. Language was not a problem in Port Richmond. Many of their new neighbors were recent immigrants from Poland, Germany, Ireland and Scotland. They all struggled with some language problem but they struggled together. Despite their varied backgrounds, they got along quite well. Most everyone could walk wherever they needed to go. On Sundays and special occasions, they could rent a horse and carriage from one of the many liveries that were scattered throughout the neighborhood and ride all the way out to Fairmount Park.

But it was tough losing two children. Eddie lived only five weeks. Lillian, who was baptized "Mary," had Bright's disease, which ruined her kidneys. She died in Charlie's arms when she was only two years old. Even the burial was difficult. Charlie and Liz couldn't afford to buy a grave but somehow a site became available in St. Dominic's Cemetery. It might have been the iron workers. It might have been a parish priest at Nativity. But the grave was there for them to use. It took nearly three hours for the horse-drawn hearse to traverse the seven miles of mostly open fields up Frankford Road to Holmesburg and the cemetery at

St. Dominic's Church on the hill beyond Pennypack Creek. People in the funeral procession packed thermoses of coffee and a bite to eat for the all-day trip. And in 1918, the Spanish Flu swept through the city killing thousands of people and lining the curbs at night with corpses that were most often buried in mass graves. Fortunately, Charlie and Liz and their seven children escaped serious illness from the Spanish Flu.

The most severe challenge came from Charlie's iron construction work. In the early 1920's, a load of steel fell from a flat car and mangled Charlie's leg, leaving him unable to work. Workers compensation was in its infancy. Railroads and other major businesses paid more attention to the useful lives of parts and equipment than they did to the lives of workmen. Workmen could be easily replaced, and without any additional cost. The new workers compensation law provided some disability payments but the checks soon stopped. Fortunately, the older children pitched in to help support the family. Times were tough, but they got by.

After the Market-Frankford Elevated was extended to northeast Philadelphia in the mid-1920's, Charlie and Liz rented a house on Howland Street, about two miles north of Port Richmond in a neighborhood called Juniata Park. It was near the route of the railroad line where factories were sprouting up. Most of the people who lived in Juniata Park worked in the nearby factories. Those were difficult times and difficult conditions but it was a damned sight better than the conditions in Conception Harbour. Liz would point out that every one of the houses she rented in Philadelphia had indoor plumbing. That could not be said for the houses in her native Newfoundland. Shed no tears for Liz. She would take this life any day of the week.

Liz's biggest challenge was one that came from Newfoundland. It was Charlie's oldest sister Nell, who they often called "Helen." In many ways, Nell was the exact opposite of Liz. Nell was well educated. Her mother and her maternal grandmother had seen to that. They were Gushues. Everyone knew that the Gushues were smart. In contrast, Liz could not read or write. Liz did not go to school. Her mother said that Liz was too ill to attend school. That was hard to figure. She was not too sick to work.

On the other hand, when Nell left Newfoundland, she was successful in the business of selling libraries to the wealthy barons of finance and industry for their mansions in Manhattan and on Philadelphia's main line. Nell never married. She enjoyed mingling with high society and her personal wealth accumulated – until the stock market crash of 1929.

Nell lost a small fortune in the stock market crash; and by that time she was 62 years of age. Her selling days were over. Still, what savings she had left was quite a lot compared to what Charlie and Liz had been able to scratch together raising a family. Liz and Charlie lived on a week-to-week basis, first on Charlie's earnings and then, after Charlie was hurt, on what their grown up children brought in. As if oblivious to this stark contrast in economic wherewithal, Nell decided that she ought to get out of her small apartment in Brooklyn and see more of her oldest brother. She became a frequent overnight visitor at the St. John household in Philadelphia.

Liz suffered these visits in relative silence while her sister-in-law would pick up the society pages of the newspaper and read aloud about the social doings of main line Philadelphians, knowing full well that Liz could not read and also knowing that Liz lacked the social graces to mingle with members of the social register. To make matters worse, Liz was expected by custom to cook meals for and generally wait on her house-guest. Conversely, Charlie's sister seemed to have the highest expectation of being waited on and

12

responded to the service much in the same way that she thought that her wealthy customers would respond to the efforts of their domestic servants. Somehow Liz controlled her temper but Nell's visits became increasingly unbearable. The situation came to a head during a particularly cold winter in the 1930's.

Some small item was needed from the store. It was bitter cold outside. The Weather Bureau did not announce the "chill factor" in those days but people had sense enough to stay indoors when the temperature dipped into the teens and below. Liz knew that she could not ask her "honored" guest to walk to the store, especially in weather like this. So, Liz got out her coat, hat, gloves and a woolen scarf and bundled up to do the job herself. The small "mom & pop" store was only about two blocks away but it felt as though it was two miles in the Antarctic. It was worse coming back. Liz was frozen to the bone. She was no youngster. All she could think of was getting back inside the house, closing the door behind her and going into the kitchen where the heat from the oven would thaw her out.

She quickened her pace as she turned the corner and neared the concrete steps up to her house. At the top of the steps, she lunged toward the doorknob – and the door was locked. How could the door be locked, she thought to herself. She was the last one out and she made sure that it was unlocked so that she could get back in. Hurriedly, she tugged the glove off her right hand and rang the doorbell. But no one answered. Again and again Liz rang the bell. She was freezing. Her feet were numb. Her face was so cold it was starting to burn. She kept ringing and ringing the doorbell. She began to think that she might freeze to death on her own front doorstep. Finally, the door opened. And there was Nell, making it clear how annoyed she was by that awful ringing of the bell; and why didn't Liz use her key?

No one knows the exact words that Liz spoke to her sister-in-law in the moments that followed. It is fairly certain that Liz's words would be understood equally as well in sixteenth century Newfoundland as in twentieth century Philadelphia. Nell never asked to have the words repeated. When Liz's daughters came home from work that evening, one of them asked, "Mom, what did you say to Aunt Nell? She's in her room crying." Liz looked straight ahead. Her face twisted slightly at the thought of the bitter cold. Her mind went back to the icy north Atlantic and the fishing schooners. Her eyes flashed and she fairly spat out the words, "The more she cries, *the less she'll have to piss!*"

You won't find that line in a Tom Hanks movie. It is from life.

BOCK'S POCONO TRAIL LODGE

Early in September 1963, Frank Reed suggested that we take a ride to the Pocono Mountains. Frank wanted to confirm arrangements he previously made for a few winter weekend vacations. He said that it would be pretty much like the social scene we had just completed in the seashore town of Margate, New Jersey. I had never been to the Poconos. Until I joined the Marine Corps in 1959, I was pretty much a stay-at-home person. This was a good chance to see what the Poconos were like.

We took the Northeast Extension of the Pennsylvania Turnpike to the Mt. Pocono Exit and then went northeast on Route 940. The intersection of Route 940 and Pennsylvania Route 115 is known as Blakeslee Corners. It was little more than a traffic light suspended over the nearly deserted crossing of two 2-lane mountain roads. About 300 yards southeast of the intersection was an old 3-story wood frame building. A sign over the front entrance declared that it was Bock's Pocono Trail Lodge.

Inside the front door was a hallway. To the right was a restaurant; to the left was a bar and lounge. The bar was curved like an elongated horseshoe with the closed end near to the center hallway. Tables and chairs were neatly spaced on each side of the bar. At the far end of the bar sat a rumpled, gray-haired man in his late sixties. He looked like Wallace Beery, a character actor from the black-and-white movies of the 1930s. He was Wilbur Bock, the owner of the premises. Wilbur sat at the end of the bar all day and all night, sometimes joined by a coterie of locals of approximately his generation. Patrons often assumed that Wilbur was something like one of Wallace Beery's characters, i.e., a dim-witted drunk with only a minimal understanding of what was going on around him. Far from it! Wilbur was a geological engineer who was retired from a high level position with the Pennsylvania agency that regulated mines. Wilbur's idea of retirement was to sit at the end of his own bar, drink his own whiskey and watch the rest of the world go by.

The business operations at Bock's were handled by Honey, Wilbur's common law wife. Honey was a short, dark-haired woman in her early fifties. She supervised the bar operations, managed the kitchen and the restaurant, and also managed the rental of the rooms on the two upper floors. Honey was a very busy lady. She had help in the operation of the bar when bartender Jimmy Butler held forth. Jimmy was in his late twenties. He had a constantly cheerful face and an uncanny ability to remember the name of everyone he met. On the other hand, some members of the kitchen staff were on the opposite end of the intelligence scale. They were mentally challenged residents of a nearby state institution. On busy weekends, Honey was stressed not only by the kitchen help but also by the need to monitor the activities of some of the lodge's unpredictable guests. Maybe that is why she was happy to make a deal with Frank McCormick and Frank Reed a year earlier.

The agreement covered five major weekends of the winter season. On those weekends, Honey would reserve all fourteen rooms in the lodge for the friends of the two Franks. The price included breakfast and dinner on Saturday. Since Honey would not have to worry about the type of people who were in the lodge, she offered a rock-bottom price. Each of the rooms could accommodate two or three persons. It worked out to about $12 per person for an entire weekend. It was a great deal. I was surprised when Frank Reed introduced me to Honey as the one who would be taking the place of Frank McCormick in coordinating the arrangement. Frank McCormick was recently married and would not be spending his weekends in the Poconos any more. In retrospect, it worked out very well. What with the popularity of the weekends and the modest price, I never had to worry about having enough people to fill all the spots and there was no difficulty getting the money in advance. Also, having been out of the Philadelphia area for the past three years, it was a great way for me to re-acquaint myself with people in my age bracket.

As Frank and I drove home that afternoon, I wondered what we would do for entertainment during a mountain weekend in that dumpy old building on Route 115. Wilbur's retirement routine was certainly not inviting. When Halloween weekend rolled around, I found out. Bock's was situated at the top of a loop of roads that ran around nearby Lake Harmony. Our days began and ended at Bock's; but in-between, we drove eight or ten miles to Lake Harmony, stopping at various locations along the way. The star of the loop was Split Rock Lodge.

Touch football at Split Rock

Split Rock was an aging star of a bygone era. It was once the executive retreat of the Lehigh Coal and Navigation Company, a corporate powerhouse in the days of "king" coal and mighty railroads. The main building was on a hill, next to the lake. Attractive stone houses dotted the lakefront to the west of the main lodge. There were ski slopes and a toboggan chute in the hills surrounding the main area of Split Rock. During the course of our weekends, we used all of those facilities at one time or another. Lehigh Coal and Navigation was no longer in control of the lodge. It sold the lodge and many of the stone houses. There was talk

17

about future development of the site as a major recreation complex.

The lodge itself looked like part of a Hollywood set. The open lobby area was rustic, built of huge logs. Trophies with plenty of antlers hung on the walls. At one end of the room there was a large fireplace with a roaring fire. Down another flight of stairs were a rectangular bar, another large fireplace, and a large room for dining and dancing. On Sunday mornings, one of the lodge's conference rooms was used as a chapel for the Catholic Mass. Monsignor Dooley would drive his motorcycle up from one of the nearby coal towns to say the Mass.

Lake Harmony Lodge was located at the other end of the lake. It was a large barn-like building, with a number of motel style cabins nearby. There was usually entertainment at Lake Harmony Lodge, but the surroundings were not in the same class as Split Rock. Between Split Rock and Lake Harmony Lodge were a number of lakefront houses, some of which were rented for the ski season by friends of ours. You can bet that they paid more than $12 for each weekend – without meals included. There were two other spots on the loop: the Sportsman's, a restaurant-motel complex near the Blakeslee Corners intersection and a bar the name of which I cannot recall, located about a mile from Bock's at the intersection of Routes 115 and 903, near the State Police Barracks.

Mary Reed Turner, Bud Sullivan, Alice Noleski, Bill Hallissey and Tom Keane

Among the Blakeslee Corners locals, Bock's Pocono Trail Lodge was the watering hole of choice. The 1960s were the days of Pennsylvania's Blue Laws. Bars were required to close at midnight on Saturdays. Bock's complied with the Blue Laws. At 12:00 midnight, the front door was locked — and the back door was opened. The lights were turned down. Everyone knew the drill. They kept the noise to a minimum. State policemen going off duty at midnight would regularly come in the back door for a drink before going home.

In the meanwhile, Bock's was our place regardless of the hour. It was where Joe Boyle and Bill Hallissey occasionally celebrated "manhattan" parties, their favorite drink – and mine too! They knew full well that their only driving obligations would be to negotiate one or two flights of stairs at the end of the evening. In the parking lot, Al Michele invariably won bets when he lifted the front ends of cars clear off the ground. In the morning, Ralph Weston took charge of the kitchen and made breakfast for anyone who was up at that hour. Honey Bock loved the arrangement.

I coordinated the schedule at Bock's for two years, even though I did not stay there during the 1964-65 winter. That year, I joined with Dick Boyle and a few others in renting a cottage on Route 903, near the "back door" to Split Rock. Still, I handled the planning and generally spent a lot of time at Bock's. One of the new people in our Bock's crowd that year was a very attractive girl named Cathy McErlean. I enjoyed being with Cathy both in the Poconos and back in Philadelphia.

My Bock's experience came to an end in September 1965, when I began evening classes at Temple University School of Law. The following June, Cathy and I were married. Cathy's family had no connection to the Pocono Mountains. The McErleans were seashore people. For

Gerry St. John and Cathy McErlean

several years, Cathy and I and our growing family spent our vacation time at the South Jersey Shore. In about 1974, we decided to try a couple of weeks in the Lake Harmony area of the Poconos. We rented a house in what was called the "Lake Harmony Estates," just below Split Rock Lodge. The cool mountain air and the slow, relaxing pace of Pocono life was a welcome change from the high temperatures and humidity of Sea Isle City. For the next ten years or so, Lake Harmony became our main vacation area.

Vacationing at Lake Harmony Estates with a wife and six children was a lot different from the $12 weekends that first brought us to the Poconos. Split Rock Lodge was not the same; it suffered a devastating fire and was rebuilt in a fashion more suitable to a modern motel complex. Also, a good bit of the open space was being developed for timeshare units and a conference center. Monsignor Dooley and his motorcycle were still there – biding his time while a new church was being built near Lake Harmony Lodge. Dooley's backwoods style had not changed. He ran a loose ship. He often said that a lot of children made their first communion when he celebrated the Mass. We were willing to take that risk with Monsignor Dooley but the same was not true with a return visit to Bock's. It was not a place that the kids would like. Moreover, they would probably resent our "forcing" them to visit such a dull place. As a result, years went by without our stopping at Bock's Pocono Trail

Lodge. Finally, I decided that this disconnect should come to an end.

Invariably, my work as a lawyer intruded on our vacation plans. Briefs had to be drafted and there was always work that had to be done during our vacation. This was in the days before the personal computer and the Internet. Buddy Segal, a senior partner, and I worked out a system where I would dictate a draft of the brief and then ship the audio-cassette to the office by Greyhound bus from the Stroudsburg bus station about 20 miles away. Buddy's secretary would type the draft and then ship it by bus to Buddy at his Longport, New Jersey condo. The changes would then be sent back to me at the Stroudsburg bus station. It worked pretty well under the circumstances, but I did find myself alone on many of those treks to and from Stroudsburg. During one of my Stroudsburg runs, I decided to stop at Bock's on my way back.

It was late afternoon; the restaurant was empty. I walked over to the bar. Jimmy Butler was behind the bar cleaning some of the glassware. I had not seen Jimmy in more than ten years. He had not changed much. He sensed my movement into the room and looked up. Without any hesitation whatever he said, "Hi Gerry, is Cathy with you?"

Jimmy filled me in on the highlights of the past decade. Honey and Wilbur finally got married. It seems that they had been on vacation in Europe when Wilbur suffered a serious accident. While he was in the hospital, Honey was out in the cold. She had absolutely no control over anything. She could not direct Wilbur's medical care or access his finances for her day-to-day living expenses. She was a bystander. When Wilbur recovered they decided to tie the knot. They became man and wife. Maybe that was not enough.

Jimmy also said that Wilbur died recently, and his children from an earlier marriage contested the will that left the business to Honey. I don't know the details of that will contest but I do know that the Pocono Trail Lodge was under new management the following year. So it happened that Bock's Lodge came to the end of its trail.

I would like to think that Honey prevailed in the will contest; but who knows? I'll bet that irascible old Wallace Beery look-alike doesn't give a damn — no matter where he is.

AGNES, A Remembrance

The following is a Remembrance, delivered at the conclusion of the funeral Mass for Agnes St. John, who died on June 18, 2010, at the age of 101 years.

Agnes was my aunt – my father's sister – as well as being my godmother. Hopefully, these memories will paint a word picture of Agnes.

Let's start with a common understanding. We have all heard it said that this is a nation of immigrants. That certainly was the case 102 years ago when Agnes was born. Her parents were immigrants; both of them came from Newfoundland. She was raised in Port Richmond – a neighborhood of immigrants. She often talked of the place on Allegheny Avenue, between Gaul and Thompson Streets, where there are three separate Catholic churches. People call those churches the German church, the Irish church, and the Polish church. According to Agnes, the rules of the neighborhood made it easy to determine your nationality. "If you spoke English, you were Irish. If you couldn't speak English, then you were German." It was as simple as that.

Agnes attended grammar school in an old gray stone building on Richmond Street. High school? She said "We weren't expected to go to high school. When we got promoted from eighth grade, we were expected to go to work and help pay the bills."

She got a job with the Liggett & Meyers, the tobacco people. She stuffed cigarettes into little packs, and she glued tops on the cardboard cartons. In 1929, she took a job in the manufacturing plant of Radio Corporation of America – RCA Victor – in Camden, New Jersey. She was a cable lacer. For the remainder of her working life, she traveled to Camden by public transportation, first by ferry and later, when the Delaware River Bridge opened, she went by the high-speed commuter line.

Agnes' limited schooling and her ethnic upbringing had a definite impact on her speech patterns. One of her favorite words, often directed at her nephews and nieces was "Divilskins," children of the devil, "the devil's kin." Closely related to Divilskins was "Divilment."

Her speech patterns would remind you of Yogi Berra. I'll give just one example. She would say, "It's best to die when you are in good health." Think about that one for a while.

Agnes was not a public figure. She had no education, no wealth, and no position of authority or importance. She lived the invisible life that is typical of people in the neighborhoods.

However, if our perspective is "service to others," then we have a different picture.

Agnes was a self-appointed surrogate mother to her nieces and nephews and to their children and grandchildren. Some of us she called "her angels." But whether or not you qualified as "an angel," Agnes was always ready to knit baby clothes, christening outfits, blankets and mittens. When she came to visit, you knew that she would bring a fresh-baked pound cake. She was a tireless housekeeper and cook. And she was an invaluable healthcare provider to her parents, brothers and sisters – and, indeed, to anyone within earshot of someone in the family.

When her brother Reds (Charles) was incapacitated by a stroke, Agnes traveled by public transportation to the East Orange, New Jersey Veterans Hospital at least two days each week to visit him. And while she was at the hospital, she would visit the other patients in the ward, bringing them cakes, cookies and conversation. When Reds was transferred to the Veterans Home in Vineland, one of the men in the East Orange ward broke down and cried – not because Reds was leaving – but because Agnes would no longer be coming to visit them. Of course, Agnes continued the same routine at the Vineland Home. And what she did for Reds was no different from what she had previously done for her father, her mother, for her sister Catherine and what she would later do for her sister Dot.

"Service to others," it is a bedrock principle of our Catholic faith. I know that Agnes would be at a complete loss to explain that principle, or any theological principle for that matter. She knew the limitations of her eighth grade education. But every so often, we read something that was said by a significant person, and it reminds us of Aunt Agnes. For example, St. Frances Cabrini was a woman who spent her life working among uneducated immigrants. She was annoyed when she heard people disparage the faith of those uneducated people. St. Frances once said:

> "The faith of the people is not to be despised. They may not be able to express the reason for their faith ... but the reasons which they possess are deeply felt in their hearts ... Everyone has a heart, the learned and the ignorant."

That almost sounds like Agnes, "Everyone has a heart, the learned and the ignorant."
And then there are the eloquent words of Venerable John Henry Newman. Cardinal Newman said:

> "God has created me to do him some definite service; he has committed some work to me

which he has not committed to another. ... I am a link in a chain, a bond of connection between persons."

Agnes was our link in the chain of the St. John family between the 19^{th,} the 20th and 21st centuries. She wasn't around in the 1800s but she had personal contact with our relatives who were around as far back as the 1840s. From 1840 to 2010, how's that for longevity?

Oliver Wendell Holmes – the poet – wrote a highly regarded poem about longevity. It is titled *"The Last Leaf."* It was said to be a favorite of Abraham Lincoln. The poem recalls an elderly, rickety old man, who was the target of many jokes of young people in Boston. They laughed at his physical appearance, his old-fashioned clothes, and his out-of-style speech. Seventy years earlier, he had been a very handsome man, one of the leaders of the famed Boston Tea Party. Holmes compares the decrepit old man to a leaf that did not fall from the tree in the autumn but instead, shriveled and bent, hung on to the tree until the following spring. The poem ends with these lines:

> "And if I should live to be
> The last leaf on the tree
> In the spring,
> Let them smile as I do now,
> At the old forsaken bough
> Where I cling."

Agnes, you done good!

A COMMON ENEMY

Prologue

Sometimes a chance remark grabs your mind and holds it hard. Such was the case one afternoon at Temple University School of Law when a well-deserved honor was being accorded to Judge Charles Klein, the President Judge of Philadelphia's Orphans' Court. Judge Klein devoted himself to the benefit of Temple University and its law school. It was a cute touch to have three of Klein's young grandchildren deliver the citation to the judge. George Forde, who was chairing the event on behalf of the Philadelphia Bar Association's Probate and Trust Section, commented that a special bond exists between grandparents and grandchildren. He then observed, "Some people say that is because they share a common enemy." It was a clever remark.

The laughter that rippled through the staid audience at the law school confirmed that the observation was one of general application. Necessarily implied by George's quip are inherent adverse relationships between parents and their children, and between children and their parents. Like stress on the spokes of a bicycle wheel, tension runs both ways. The youthful quest for control of one's own affairs brings us directly to the boundaries established by our parents, the lines beyond which we dare not tread. The mutual resistance of those two opposing parties makes them adversaries or, to use another word, "enemies." And the interaction of love, duty, honor, insistence, resistance and self-determination makes it almost impossible for the simultaneous perceptions of parent and child to coincide.

I cannot accurately describe my father. Dad was the 700-pound gorilla; an authority figure with a command voice that seemed to come from beyond the clouds and a propensity to inflict rather than administer corporal punishment. That image is in stark contrast to the impression conveyed by the stack of black-and-white photographs of the distinguished gentleman with the engaging smile. It would also contrast sharply with the perceptions of his many friends and acquaintances throughout the Philadelphia area. He was well liked.

Admittedly, some of my less than flattering perceptions may have been shaped by the less than enjoyable circumstances that surrounded some of those occurrences. For example, one function of the male parent is to serve escort duty on unpleasant occasions such as visits to the pain emporiums of dentists. One such instance involved a molar extraction by a center city practitioner who advertised himself on the radio as Dr. "Singing Sam" Algase. His offices were across the street from Wanamaker's at 13th and Market Streets. Algase sang his own commercial jingle in which he admonished his listeners to "wear a sunny smile." After my encounter with Singing Sam, I wore a bloody countenance. On the way home I used an old hubcap that Dad found in the trunk of the car as a spittoon for the excess blood. I never forgot Singing Sam. Hey Sam, here's your sunny smile!

And then there were Dad's tours of Philadelphia. He had a mailman's perspective of history. We learned that Benjamin Franklin was the first Postmaster General of the United States and that another Postmaster General, John Wanamaker, was the one who began parcel post service. Parcel post began its operations at the same time that Mr. Wanamaker opened his new department store across the street from that damnable dentist. Near the Delaware River, we learned that the historic colonial houses had large courtyards and gardens in the back and that many of those backyards had out-houses that were still in use. We were glad that he did not take us there in the summer.

We seemed to be part of a lecture circuit. It would generally begin with the words, "When I was a boy . . .." What followed did not necessarily have any relevance to any point of immediate interest and the conclusion was usually that we should do something that Dad had chosen not to do himself. However, there were times when we were urged to follow his example and not undertake activities that he thought were lacking in value. Sports was an example. Some parents are criticized for trying to relive their childhood athletic dreams through their children. Far from it.

We struggled for the opportunity to achieve our own athletic dreams in our own time. St. Paul might have been surprised to learn that when he wrote about "putting away the things of a child," he was referring to his baseball glove. After all, now that we were in high school we should "stop playing games" or, now that we were in college we should . . . or, now that we were out of college . . .. Well, you get the picture. Eventually, we reached an accommodation. We continued to play ball and Dad continued to treat it as a waste of time. The overwhelming urge to prove him wrong is just one of the emotional forces that distort objectivity and make rational assessment impossible.

Perhaps the only way fairly to describe a parent is to use the device suggested by St. Ignatius for decision-making and view the parent as an unrelated person, say as a close friend similarly situated in all relevant respects. In such an exercise, one might say something like the following.

Men of Iron

John was the second child of Charlie and Liz St. John who lived in Nativity parish in Philadelphia. He was their second child but the first son. Someone told Liz that King Alfonso of Spain had offered to give a ring to every child born in 1904 who was named Alfonso. That was good enough for Liz. The boy was baptized John Alfonso St. John. A few months later, the ring came in the mail. They thought that it was a good omen. But it was not long before someone stole the ring off the baby's finger when he was sleeping in his stroller. Whoever took the ring might as well have taken his middle name too. Nearly all of his records created later in life would show the letters "NMN," meaning "No Middle Name." For a while, even the "John" disappeared. His family called him "Jack."

Jack was the center of attraction at the St. John house on Chatham Street in the Port Richmond neighborhood. In the next few years, two more daughters would be born but Jack was the St. Johns' only son for a full six years until Santa Claus dropped off little Charles, the red head, on Christmas Day in 1910. By that time, Jack had started first grade at Nativity Church's grammar school.

School was a challenge that Jack did not relish. He was bright enough and energetic enough. But he had no interest in class work. He was outspoken to the point of being confrontational. His main interest was getting a job, which would mean that he would have spending money and first-rate clothes. He knew from his father that there were many jobs available in ironwork and that the pay was good. His father did not like the idea but Jack persisted. On his last day of class in eighth grade, Jack got into a heated argument with his teacher and walked out of class. After a conference between the Mother Superior and Jack's parents, it was decided that Jack would be permitted to graduate. But he did not care one way or the other. He had no intention of continuing school.

It was not difficult for a fourteen year old to find work. World War I was winding down but it still fueled the economy. Automobiles and motor driven trucks were becoming almost as common as horse carts on Philadelphia's cobblestone streets and crowned dirt roads. The railroads were in the process of electrification and light rail trolleys were being used increasingly throughout the city. There was even talk about building an elevated train line that would take people into center city, "downtown," and back. Ironworkers were in demand. Jack joined his father on the job. He was fascinated by the work. The building trades had always been a mystery. Now he found that the way things were built and the way that those things worked were matters of common sense. They could be learned. The important thing was to think the job through.

Charlie still did not like the idea of his boy working in iron construction. It was too demanding and too dangerous. He told Jack about his own childhood on the fishing schooners in the north Atlantic off Newfoundland, and how boats and men were lost in storms, fog and icy water. He told his son of the dangers in building a railroad on Newfoundland and in completing the western section of the Canadian Pacific's transcontinental line. Charlie came to this country to do better and he thought that his son could do better still. His pleas were to no avail.

A few years later, the father's point was made the hard way. There was nothing different or unusual about that day. Jack got his work assignment early in the morning and went off with one of the job crews. That was to be expected. The new workers were assigned to the jobs that the old-timers did not want. Sometimes it was because the job was especially difficult. Sometimes it was because of the inconvenient location of the job. Jack knew that was the way that things were done. That was fine with him. He was making good money. So long as they paid him, he would go where he was told and do whatever job the other workers would do.

When his crew returned to the yard that afternoon, Jack sensed immediately that something was wrong. There had been an accident. A shipment of steel was being unloaded from a flatcar. The load shifted, and then without warning spilled off the car. Charlie was directly in the path of the steel. He did not have a chance. Charlie's leg was mangled. His days as an ironworker were ended.

As Jack walked home from the hospital that evening, he thought about the future. Charlie's words had not conveyed the harsh reality of ironwork, the railroads or the fishing schooners. To Jack, those dangers were not real. But now, this was real. Some people said that Charlie was lucky because a new worker's compensation law had been passed and he would receive disability checks for a few years. Old-timers said that in their day, the workers were simply written off with no compensation at all.

"T'ank God he's alive," said Jack's mother. They all knew that finances would be tight. Jack was surprised at how easily his mother adjusted to the setback. The more he thought about the accident, the more Jack became convinced that he would get out of iron work. His first step was to take night classes in math and mechanical drawing at Temple University and general studies at Northeast High School.

Neither Snow nor Rain nor Gloom of Night . . . .

On February 15, 1924, Jack started a new job as a substitute mail carrier in the United States Post Office. The new job brought with it a uniform, including a durable leather bag with a shoulder strap, and a pay rate of 60 cents per hour. In the 1920's, substitute carriers had to be available for work at any of the post offices anywhere in the city. About six years experience was required before a substitute could be expected to reach the full-time level of "regular carrier." One of the prerequisites to becoming a "regular" was learning the post office "scheme," i.e., the location of every street in Philadelphia and the post office that served every street address. Zip codes did not exist but there were numbers assigned to each postal substation. These were known as "zone numbers." For example, Frankford Station was zone 24. Holmesburg Station was zone 36. People sometimes put the zone on their letters but regular postal employees were required to know the right zone number regardless of whether or not it was shown on the address. Jack had no problem learning the scheme. In fact, he enjoyed the opportunity of walking through every part of Philadelphia.

Jack St. John

Jack's walking was temporarily suspended in 1925 when he was involved in an automobile accident and fractured the base of his spine. However, it was not long before he was back on the mail routes. At about that time, he enrolled in a one-semester real estate course at Temple University. Philadelphia was enjoying a building boom. Major building projects underway at the time included the Benjamin Franklin Parkway, the Museum of Art, the Public Ledger Building, and the Delaware River Bridge to name just a few. Builders had learned how to fireproof steel girders, and skyscrapers began to spring up in the downtown area. From the looks of things, there would be profitable opportunities in real estate, either on a part-time basis while working as a substitute carrier or, perhaps, in full-time real estate sales.

When the stock market crashed in 1929, the idea of selling real estate effectively came to an end. Businesses closed their doors and employees were thrown out of work without any type of unemployment compensation. Few people had any money to buy real estate. His friends told Jack that he was lucky to be working for the federal government. Those were among the few jobs available during the depression and they were special in that they maintained the same pay level as before the crash. By 1931, Jack was making $2,100 per year as a full time letter carrier. He was glad that he had the job. And he was glad that he had enough money to lend $500 to his sister Katherine and her husband Jim Shanley to make their mortgage payments while Jim was out of work. He also had enough money to buy a car. Was he lucky? Maybe. Jack liked being a letter carrier.

Jack even enjoyed the early starting time. He had to be at the station by 4:30 in the morning. The city was a different place at that hour of the morning. Typically, he would leave the house at about 4:00 a.m. and drive to the post office. It was very quiet. There was no traffic. He had the streets almost to himself. The only other movement was an occasional milkman. In that era, milk was delivered right to the door. Each of the major dairies had a fleet of wagons or trucks that worked residential routes and delivered milk and cream in glass bottles to the customers' front steps in the early morning. The milkmen used wire hand-baskets to carry as many bottles as possible, constantly returning to the truck with the empties that people left out on the step the night before. In the days of the horse and wagon, the milkman and the horse worked as a team. As the milkman made his front step deliveries, the horse followed along the curbside at the same pace, so that the wagon was always right at hand. But trucks had neither memory nor initiative. Milkmen quickly developed a routine of stopping their trucks smack in the middle of the street. There was no need to pull over to the curb. No one else was on the street at that hour of the morning.

The white trucks parked in the middle of the street with their lights on and their engines running reminded Jack of his father's stories of icebergs drifting in the path of fishing schooners in the north Atlantic. They looked peaceful but many a schooner was broken to pieces by those gigantic islands of ice. The peaceful milk trucks also presented a deceptive danger as Jack soon learned when he started to pass one. Without any warning at all, a white coated figure with a wire basket in each hand leaped from the open doorway of the truck right across the path of Jack's car. The milkman never hesitated. He was in full stride and went right on making his deliveries. He was used to having the street to himself in the morning. Jack made it a habit to give milk trucks a wide berth on his way to work.

Letter carriers started their day by sorting out the mail in the same sequence as the addresses along the mail route. The sorting process was done at a desk on which was mounted what looked like a large bookcase with about seven shelves. The shelves had vertical slots, one for each address on the route. It took about two or three hours, depending on the number of addresses, to "case up the route," and then Jack would be in the neighborhoods while children were going to school and local businesses were starting their day. Jack enjoyed the easy banter with the people on his route. He learned something about them, about their businesses, their homes and their neighborhoods. On one occasion there was an automobile accident. A youngster on the way to school had been hit by a car. He was not badly hurt but he was pinned underneath the car so that if the vehicle moved it would crush the boy. It would be a while before a hoist could get to the scene and lift the car. The boy was becoming increasingly frightened. Jack lay down in the street beside where the boy was caught. He slid the leather mailbag under the car and told the youngster to use it as a pillow. Meanwhile, Jack lay there talking to the boy until the hoist arrived. That done, Jack finished delivering the mail.

It was in 1931 that he joined the United States Marine Corps Reserve. It was an interesting experience. The reserve unit spent most of its time taking Marine Corps Institute correspondence courses in English and mathematics. Jack was surprised that such a rugged military organization would emphasize schooling. He had expected that the emphasis would be on physical fitness. However, there was a two-week field exercise at the Marine Corps Base in Quantico, Virginia. Jack enjoyed the exercise. And he liked what he saw of Quantico. He rose to the rank of corporal but he did not have enough free time to keep up with the time commitments that the reserve required.

Jack was dating Betty Metzinger, a short, dark-haired telephone operator who worked for the Bell Telephone Company of Pennsylvania. She was five years older than Jack. Betty had been living on her own for more than a dozen years, even before her mother died of the flu in 1920. Officially, the Spanish Flu Epidemic of 1918 had come to an end well before 1920, but the official termination date did not help Mary Crowley Metzinger. Betty's father was a foreman at the John B.

Jack and Betty St. John

Stetson factory at 7th and Master Streets. Betty's sister Edna was married to Joe McLoughlin, a photo engraver who lived in North Philadelphia. Betty was smart. Off and on she had attended college classes at Temple University.

Betty also liked to cook. She had a special talent for baking. Jack and Betty would talk, sometimes in jest sometimes seriously, about starting a business together. In February 1931, they almost did just that. Harvey Knauer had a small baked goods business in the Roxborough section of the city. Business was slow and Knauer hoped to be able to sell the assets to some susceptible entrepreneur. They worked out a deal. Knauer would sell Harvey's Home Made Pie Baking Co. to Jack and his partner, Howard Briew. Betty would handle the baking and Jack would handle sales and delivery. The Tastykake Company needn't have worried about the competition. The enterprise never got off the ground. However, on December 17, 1932, Jack and Betty entered into another type of contract in a nuptial Mass celebrated at the Cathedral of Saints Peter and Paul.

In December 1933, there was a tragic accident in the McLoughlin family. Edna's son, Joey, was nearly twelve years old. He was playing "cops and robbers" with his friends. One of the boys added realism to the game by using his father's police revolver. They did not know that the revolver was loaded. Everyone was surprised by the loud bang. The bullet hit Joey in the back. The surgeons at the hospital knew that there was not much that they could do for him. Joey hung on for three months. The injury devastated Joey's family. His father could not bear to go to Joey's hospital room. But Jack went to the hospital. He went there every day, talking to Joey much the way that he had talked to the youngster under the automobile a few years earlier. He and Joey made plans for the things that they would do when Joey got out of the hospital. But Joey didn't make it. He died in

March 1934. Jack felt like he lost a member of his own family.

Jack became more active in the mail carriers' labor union, the National Association of Letter Carriers. He ran for the office of treasurer of the Keystone Branch and was ecstatic when he was elected. He quickly became friends with the other officers of the branch, particularly Ray Thomas and Phil Convery. Ray Thomas seemed to know his way around the post office and the inner circle of the union. Jack was convinced that Thomas was destined for big things in the Philadelphia post office. As officers of the Keystone Branch, the three men represented Philadelphia's mail carriers at conventions and union meetings in Kansas City, Cleveland, Boston, Pittsburgh and New York City. Jack was beginning to learn that there was much that he did not know about labor relations and about running an organization. He had not realized that one responsibility of the treasurer would be to organize the annual dinners for the membership and for the union's leadership. He was fortunate to have a high energy level. Jack had to deal with the downtown hotels in Philadelphia and he had to account for the use of the local's money. He was learning on the job.

Jack was also learning about the demands of family life. His first son was born on Columbus Day, October 12, 1934. There was no question but that the boy would be named John. A second son arrived two years later on December 8, 1936. But this time there were mixed emotions. Betty was hemorrhaging badly and might not survive. As was common in those days when childbirth was a much riskier proposition, "worst case scenario" plans were made for raising the children. Young Jack would be raised by Jack's mother. The new baby would be raised by Katherine and Jim Shanley. Fortunately, Betty recovered and Jack discovered that part of the deal was that the second son would be named for Saint Gerard Majella, the patron saint of expectant mothers. Jack would have preferred Tim, or Mike, but no one asked for his opinion. He also did not have too much time to think about it. His father had recently been diagnosed with throat cancer.

The medical profession could not do much with cancer in the 1930's. Their main approach seemed to be to cut away the affected tissue. It was a process of trial and error. It was done without an effective painkiller. It was a terrible ordeal for Charlie St. John. And it was tough on Jack too. Jack had never been particularly religious but he felt his faith in a merciful God ebbing away. How could God let this suffering happen? In August 1937, Charlie was admitted to Philadelphia General Hospital. When Jack came to visit, Charlie told Jack to bring the car, that he wanted to go home. The attending physicians were vehemently opposed but Charlie signed himself out and Jack took him home. They brought a chair from the dining room out to the curb. Charlie sat on the chair and they carried him and the chair up the steps and into the house. Charlie died before noon the next day.

Jack's mail route in the Olney Post Office gave him an excellent opportunity to keep track of the housing available in Philadelphia, particularly in the northeast. Unlike many of the letter carriers in the post office, Jack did not favor the established row house neighborhoods of West Philadelphia. He had delivered mail throughout the farm areas of Holmesburg, Bustleton and Rhawnhurst, and he thought that the houses being built in those areas were far superior to the houses in older parts of the city both in quality and in terms of open space for recreation and space for automobiles. Jack and Betty narrowed their interest to a row of homes that was being built in the 3400 block of Chippendale Avenue, near Pennypack Park. That was where they would buy their new house.

The exercise of determining where they would buy their house reawakened the skills that Jack had learned at the real estate courses he had taken at Temple University a dozen years earlier. After making a few calculations, he went to see his father's oldest sister, Helen, at her apartment in Brooklyn. Helen had money. She had loaned Katherine and Jim Shanley the money for the down payment on their house in Juniata Park a few years before. Jack told Aunt Helen about the development on Chippendale Avenue and about the rows that were to be built on the north side of the street and on both sides of the 3300 block. The corner house at 3400 Chippendale had already been sold. Jack suggested that Helen buy the other three corner houses at a price of about $7,000 each, and that she convert them into 3-unit rental properties. She could live in one of the units and rent the other eight. That would provide her with a very good income. It was an attractive opportunity. But Helen had lost a small fortune in the stock market crash of 1929, and that money had been in banks and in blue chip stocks. She could not risk losing the money that remained. She could not afford to take another hit.

The opportunity was lost. In retrospect, it was an excellent suggestion. The corner houses were in great demand and eventually three of the four corners were converted into rental units, providing their owners with steady streams of income. Twenty-three years later, when Helen St. John went to her final reward, the corner houses had tripled in value. But Helen could not make investments based on 20/20 hindsight.

Jack had a regular routine of checking on the progress of construction of the new house. At the end of each workday he would drive to Chippendale Avenue and inspect the work that had been done that day. It was the last row of development to the north. Beyond Chippendale Avenue were open fields and farms for half a mile up to Holmesburg and then more open fields beyond. Holmesburg was an old community. Thomas Holme had been William Penn's surveyor, the one who originally drew up the grid-like plan for Penn's "Green Country Town." One block to the west of the 3400 block of Chippendale Avenue was the edge of Pennypack Park and, on the hill about 500 yards away, was the old poor house farm that had been built to serve Lower Dublin Township in an earlier time, before the township disappeared in the consolidation of city and county. The farm consisted of a large stone building, two barns, a pasture and a large cornfield. It was a wonderful combination of city and country.

Jack put his early knowledge of construction to good use. He was particularly interested in the insulation under the roof of the house that was being built on Chippendale Avenue. In the fading light of the late afternoon, he pulled himself up to the opening in the upstairs bedroom closet and assured that the contractor had indeed filled the entire space with rock wool insulation from the ceiling beams up to the roof. Thirty years later he would lose a bet to an insulation salesman who cut an opening in the roof and showed Jack how insulation had been piled high only around the closet opening but was in a thin layer everywhere else under the broad expanse of roof. Obviously, the building contractor knew a thing or two about cutting costs and about dealing with prospective purchasers who thought they knew something about construction.

The house on Chippendale Avenue gave Jack plenty of opportunity to practice his mechanical skills. Sometimes with the assistance of his next-door neighbor, Tom Crossley, and sometimes with the help of his brother-in-law Ralph Peyton, and sometimes on his own, he upgraded the electrical wiring, realigned the plumbing, installed a powder room, patched the roof, painted and papered the entire house, and widened the garage. He hired a master plumber to move the water, gas and heating pipes in the basement but he did not like the way the job was done. He paid the plumber, and then disassembled the entire job and re-did it himself.

Jack and Betty settled on the house at 3406 Chippendale Avenue in the first week of May 1939. The purchase price was $5,290.00. Shortly after settlement, they moved in with their growing family. The move came barely a month after the arrival of their daughter. Patricia was born on March 20th. Again there was a discussion about the name and this time Jack had his say. The baby was baptized Elizabeth Patricia, which later became E. Patricia or, more often, just plain Patricia or Pat.

Jack St. John with Gerard and Patricia

Brother Alfred

Jack was glad to move into the new house. He needed the added space now that he was in a classroom setting once again. He had recently enrolled in the Sunday Labor-Management School at La Salle College. The school was conducted under the direction of Brother E. Alfred, FSC, A.M., LL.D., President Emeritus of La Salle College. Brother Alfred was concerned about socialist influences in American labor unions. He wanted to assure that American labor leaders were equal to the challenges that were facing them. Policemen, firemen, teamsters, stevedores and representatives of business and industry were invited to participate in Sunday morning classes in leadership, psychology, practical English, labor problems and public speaking. Local radio stations donated free time on Sunday evenings for discussions, debates and public service announcements by members of the Labor-Management School. The program was a huge success and Jack was an active part of it.

La Salle College had a beautiful campus. The two main buildings formed a right angle at the southeast corner of 20th Street and Olney Avenue. The buildings were four stories high with sharply pitched slate roofs. On the interior of the property was a landscaped quadrangle. Set back from the south side of the quadrangle was another brick building, taller than the others but more square, almost squat in appearance. The squat building housed La Salle's gymnasium. Its south door opened onto a quarter-mile cinder track and a football field with stadium seats on both sides. The year after Jack enrolled, a smaller brick building was added to the east side of the quadrangle to provide needed classroom and residence space.

From his vantage point at the Olney Post Office, Jack had watched the campus emerge from a wooded hillside on the outskirts of Germantown to its present state of development. It had been a part of the Wister Estate, also known as Belfield. The Belfield property was one of those large "summer estates" owned by well-to-do Philadelphians in colonial times. It had not been touched by the growth of industry in Philadelphia. In about 1926, the Christian Brothers decided that a portion of the Belfield property would be a perfect place to relocate their college which had outgrown its old quarters at Broad and Stiles Streets, near center city Philadelphia. When the Sunday Labor-Management School began in 1938, the campus was just nine years old. Jack thought that it looked the way that a college campus should look.

But Jack was not the kind of person to be moved by appearances alone. The thing about La Salle that most impressed Jack was the founder of its labor-management school, Brother Alfred. Short in stature, with an angelic face and a snow-white goatee, Brother Alfred was a proven leader. He was brilliant. In addition to his teaching responsibilities, Brother Alfred had served as president of three colleges, two in Washington D.C. and La Salle. He was largely responsible with builder John McShain for the construction of La Salle's buildings at the 20th and Olney campus. Brother Alfred also had a well-established reputation as a labor arbitrator, respected by both unions and management. He had the ability to inspire people. And Jack was one of those he inspired. An even more critical measure of Brother Alfred's influence was the view of Betty St. John. Betty held Jack's friends to a very high standard, a standard that few of them could meet. "Jack's a better friend of theirs than they are of his," she would often say. But "Brother Al" was in a class by himself. In Betty's opinion, Brother Alfred was "a charming man." She observed that his first words in every conversation were to compliment her appearance or a piece of jewelry that she was wearing. "He just made you feel good to be in his company," she said.

The respect and admiration worked both ways. Brother Alfred recognized Jack's innate ability and he urged Jack to enroll in an accredited college program and to get a bachelor's degree. Brother Alfred explained that education greatly increases the effectiveness of a talented person. Jack told himself that he did not have sufficient time available to achieve that goal. The truth was that Jack was afraid that he would not do well in a classroom setting. He had not liked school and he had peremptorily walked out at the end of eighth grade. Now, he was beginning to realize the need for leadership psychology and communication skills, which could be best acquired through higher education. But Jack worried about whether he could carry his own weight in competition with real students. He was not a bookish person. Jack favored the spoken word. He put off his decision on college and focused on the labor-management program. After a few years, Jack thought that too much time had passed by for him to begin taking college courses. But he took Brother Al's advice to heart with respect to his children. He made up his mind that the children would attend college.

    As the children approached school age, both Jack and Betty agreed that they would attend Catholic schools. In the 1940's, there was no tuition in the parochial schools. All of the teachers were nuns who dedicated their lives to teaching, mainly in the grammar schools. Most Catholics, having no economic coercion to force them into public schools, sent their children to the parish schools. The Archdiocese of Philadelphia insisted on attendance at Catholic schools. It might have been a byproduct of a latent anti-Catholic sentiment that lay barely below the surface of Philadelphia society and it might have been the decidedly Protestant orientation of the public schools, but Catholics were warned to avoid non-Catholic schools and non-Catholic churches for fear of giving *scandal*. Betty did not go along with that theory. When Reverend King, the minister of the United Presbyterian Church, who lived directly across the back driveway, invited the neighborhood children to attend his summer "Bible school," Betty quickly gave her permission. "They teach pretty much the same thing as we do. It won't hurt the children to read the Bible in their school," she said.

    At home, Jack found the opportunity to develop some of the social graces that he had observed in his travels and in the organization of group dinners. Proper table manners were the rule of the house. Through practice, Jack developed a high level of skill carving roasts and poultry at the dinner table. At holiday dinners with his mother, sisters and brothers, as well as his own family, Jack would station himself at the center of the table and, with a flourish, carve individual slices to the order of each person. It was a professional performance. And he enjoyed performing.

Jack was also right at home in the public speaking part of La Salle's program. His affirmative manner and high energy level were good fits with public speaking. Brother Alfred taught him the proper way to prepare a speech and how to address a large audience. The preparation for his talks also increased Jack's knowledge of and interest in history and English. One of his topics was the role of the United States Post Office. In preparing these remarks, Jack learned that the post office's motto had been borrowed from Herodotus' fourth century B.C. description of the couriers who served the King of Persia; that Benjamin Franklin had run very efficient postal operations for the colonies and later for the United States; and that Buffalo Bill Cody held the non-stop distance record for riders of the legendary Pony Express that carried the mail from St. Joseph, Missouri to San Francisco, California in 1860.

In the 1930's, there were no television sets. Radio was the popular form of family entertainment. In the evenings, families would gather around a large console radio in the living room and listen to their favorite programs. Family and friends were impressed when they heard Jack speaking over the radio on Sunday evenings. The new found interest in history also prompted Jack to save items that he thought would have historical significance such as the newspapers published on the day that war was declared and propaganda texts distributed by Nazi Germany giving accounts of atrocities allegedly committed by Poland against its German minority population. Jack's prior experience organizing dinners came in handy when he was asked to handle the dinner functions of the school and its affiliated organizations, the La Salle College Civic and Social Congress, and The American Congress for Civic, Social and Industrial

Achievement. They used the names of those two organizations interchangeably.

Brother Alfred knew the value of publicity. He established the De La Salle Medal to recognize the cause of industrial peace. Brother Alfred wanted the medal to be presented to very important persons. Nothing succeeds like success. An award that is shared by the most important men in America would be seen by everyone as a very significant award. Brother Alfred announced that the first recipient would be the President of the United States, Franklin Delano Roosevelt. Working through Congressman James P. McGranery, a member of the De La Salle group, Brother Alfred arranged to present the medal to the president in his office in Washington, D.C.

On January 8, 1941, Jack found himself walking through the front door of the White House and down a long corridor

President Roosevelt, the first recipient of the De La Salle medal, shown at the White House. Reading from left to right: President Roosevelt, James P. McGranery, the Assistant to the U. S. Attorney General, and former Congressman; Brother Alfred, presenting the medal; Philip Convery, Assistant Superintendent of Mails, and John St. John, Treasurer of the La Salle College Congress.

toward a desk that was situated to the side of a large door. "Can I help you gentlemen?" the woman at the desk asked. She was the first person at the White House to inquire about the nature of their business. Jim McGranery spoke, "We're here to see the president to present the De La Salle Medal. We have an appointment." Scanning her desk calendar quickly, the woman said, "Oh yes, go right in gentlemen. The president is expecting you." It did not occur to Jack until many years later that a president might require more stringent personal protection on a daily basis. The next fifteen minutes flew by almost as if it had never happened. The president was gracious, and Brother Alfred and Congressman McGranery were equal to the task. A photographer appeared as if out of nowhere. They all smiled.

One person who was not smiling was His Eminence Dennis Cardinal Dougherty, Archbishop of Philadelphia. Cardinal Dougherty had been watching the progress of the Sunday labor-management program and he was not entirely happy with what he saw. More to the point, he was not happy with what he was hearing. And what he was hearing were complaints from some of the largest contributors to the Archdiocese. They complained to Dougherty that Brother Alfred and La Salle College were taking the side of the labor unions against the management of the businesses owned by those substantial contributors. They wanted to know whether the Cardinal could do anything about that situation. There was plenty that the Cardinal could do.

Under the college's charter, the Archbishop was the chairman of the board of directors. Cardinal Dougherty ordered La Salle College to shut down the labor-management school. Brother Alfred was transferred to the Christian Brothers Normal Institute at Ammendale, Maryland to live out his life in retirement. Brother Alfred obeyed those directives. But he continued to communicate with Jack and other members of the De La Salle group by mail, urging them to continue the work for industrial peace. It was almost by remote control from Ammendale that the De La Salle Medal was presented to industrialist Henry Kaiser, albeit without any fanfare.

In January 1941, it was business as usual at the Stetson hat factory in north Philadelphia. Foreman John Metzinger kept a close check on the pace of production on his line. An easy-going man, he joked with the workers as he walked through the busy plant. He stopped and told his assistant to keep an eye on things while he took a short break. The other man nodded his assent. John turned toward the rest room area and, without any warning, crumpled to the floor. The workmen left their stations and rushed to his aid. It was no use. John Metzinger was dead. Although he was only 64 years old, he had outlived two wives. The company quickly notified Edna McLoughlin and Betty St. John, his only surviving children.

Early that same evening, Edna and Betty arrived at their father's house at 3354 Disston Street. They were surprised to see that the lights were on both upstairs and down. When they entered the front door, one of their cousins, and then another, came down the front stairs from the bedrooms. Each was carrying one of the lamps that belonged on the bureau in the front bedroom. The cousins blurted out their condolences and said that they had come over "to make sure that everything was alright." They said that they were taking the lamps "to remember your father by." That said, they walked out of the house. Betty was furious. She locked the door and then she and Edna went through the entire house to see if anything else was missing.

After the funeral, Edna and Betty sat down at their father's dining room table and divided the estate between them. They had already agreed that Edna would take the house. Betty took the bedroom set and other pieces of furniture. When dividing the jewelry, Betty looked for items like her father's diamond stickpin that she could pass along to her sons as a continuing memento. But the predominant memory of that sad occasion would be that of finding the cousins looting her father's house within a few hours of his death. Throughout her life, Betty would warn her friends after a death in the family to lock all of the doors and make a detailed inventory.

It was not long after the Estate of John F. Metzinger, Deceased, was settled that the country found itself in the Second World War. Most of the families on Chippendale Avenue were approximately the same age. The heads of the households were too old for military service and their children were too young. There were exceptions. Two houses away, Don Rickard was young enough to serve in the navy. Next door, Jim and Mary Wilson's son Bud was eighteen. He went into the army. Three years later, Bud Wilson was killed when a transport plane crashed into the side of a mountain in Italy. Jack's brother Reds was already in the army at the outbreak of the war and Bill soon joined the Marines. But for most of the families on Chippendale Avenue, the war meant mainly shortages of almost everything that money could buy. Ration stamps were issued for gasoline and liquor. There were ration cards and, later, coins issued by the OPA (the Office of Price Administration) for meat and other food items. And even if you had sufficient ration stamps, that did not guarantee that any stores would have the items that you wanted. Things were in short supply.

On occasion, farmers from the area, and sometimes from nearby New Jersey, would park a truck in an open lot on Frankford Avenue and sell loaves of bread or farm products. Word of those sales spread like wildfire through the neighborhood and there would soon be a long line of people waiting for a chance to buy a loaf or two. When the product was butter or meat, it sold out in record time. If you saw that there was a line, you were too late. It was already gone. Local butchers looked to their friends and relatives who operated farms for fresh meat. Private enterprise flourished. If you knew a butcher who had good contacts with local farmers, you cultivated his friendship. If the butcher who had the contacts was someone that you did not know, you called him part of the "black market." It was more of a nuisance than a hardship; almost as if the entire country was on a diet.

Politics as Usual

Cardinal Dougherty may have closed its doors but the labor-management school brought home to Jack the importance of politics in a representative democracy. He began to view political activity as a civic duty, a matter of social responsibility. And La Salle also brought him into close contact with people involved in government and politics. By and large, Jack liked the people that he met at La Salle. One of his closest friends was a large congenial La Salle grad named John Byrne. Jack knew the Byrnes from their taproom on Delaware Avenue in the Fishtown section of Philadelphia. It was a frame building with a metal covering on the outside; hence its name, "The Tin Brick." It was a popular spot with the truck drivers who worked the piers and the nearby warehouses. Byrne was taking over the family business and he was also active in politics in the expanding northeast part of Philadelphia. Another friend named Bill Green was also active in politics in the northeast.

Jack now found himself in the company of many men who were younger than he. Jack was 34 years of age when the Sunday labor-management program began and many of the other participants were in their mid-twenties. Maybe that is why his name began to change. More and more of his younger acquaintances were calling him "John." And he really didn't mind being called "John." In a way, it helped him accept the fact that he was getting older. At the start of the Second World War, he volunteered for active duty in the postal section of the military service but was turned down because of age and family status. He told himself that the rejection letter was addressed to "John" St. John, not Jack. Maybe the La Salle people had it right. Jack, . . . "John" . . . made up his mind that he would do what he could to help the political success of his young friends.

Supporting the political success of John's friends proved more difficult than it first appeared. In northeast Philadelphia's Fifth Congressional District, the elected representative was almost always a member of the Republican Party. John and his friends were Democrats. But the northeast was growing and the Democrats were making inroads into the Republicans' registration lead. In the meanwhile, John Byrne and Bill Green reached a "gentleman's agreement" whereby they would take turns as the Democratic candidate for congress in the fifth district. In 1942, Green was the unsuccessful candidate but the election was very close. Hopes began to rise for success in 1944. That would be John Byrne's turn to run. Everyone knew that if Byrne won in 1944, he would continue to hold the office unless defeated and the most likely prospect was that his hold on the office would become even stronger over time. Green saw the 1944 election in practical terms as his last chance at congressional office. He knew that the Democratic candidate would be exceptionally strong running in the year of a presidential election with Franklin Roosevelt as the party's presidential candidate. Green seized the opportunity and announced his candidacy for congress in the primary election. He challenged John Byrne and repudiated the "agreement" that both of them had honored for years.

John was stunned by the sudden enmity between his two friends. He did not relish the prospect of having to choose between them. On the other hand, there was no real question as to which candidate he would support. John knew about the gentleman's agreement and thought that it should be honored. Besides, John Byrne was his closest friend. John threw all of his energy into Byrne's campaign for congress. It soon became clear, if it had not been clear before, that Bill Green was a very astute politician. Green immediately approached the party regulars and sought their support for his campaign. He was able to recruit many of them by his direct approach. But his most effective politicking may have been in his dealings with the workers like John, the ones who remained loyal to Byrne. To these workers Green said, "I understand your decision. And I admire your loyalty to John Byrne. But don't forget that I am the guy on the other side. Don't try too hard to beat my head in." It was good psychology. Many of Byrne's workers gave only a half-hearted effort. Green won the primary and became the party's candidate in the 1944 election.

No sooner was the primary over than Bill Green approached Byrne in an effort to make amends before the November election. To win the election against the Republican candidate, Green needed Byrne and his supporters. It would be almost impossible to win if Byrne's workers opposed him. And Green knew that Byrne was miffed, and with good reason. A friend of both men, John found himself being drawn into the discussions. Gradually they worked out the terms of a peace treaty. One part of the deal proposed by Green was that if he won the congressional seat he would take Byrne's friend John to Washington with him as his executive secretary. It was an outstanding opportunity. But John thought about his father's unexpected accident so many years ago, and the unexpected depression, and the absolutely certain needs of his young family. He had twenty years invested in the post office and it offered security. Also, while he liked and respected Bill Green, the relationship was not the same as it was with Byrne. John told Green and Byrne that he could not go along with this part of the proposal but that he would do whatever he could for Green's campaign. In the end, Green and Byrne made peace with each other and Bill Green went on to win the congressional election in the fifth district and took his seat in congress in January 1945.

After the war ended in 1945, large numbers of servicemen returned home and many of them sought jobs in the post office. For the first time, African Americans entered the postal service in substantial numbers. As would be expected, they became members of the letter carriers union. John continued to be active in the union leadership and he continued to undertake responsibility for the union's annual dinners. But now there was a new element in the equation. The catering manager of the large downtown hotel was completing the arrangements for the dinner when he made an almost off-hand comment that "of course, your colored members cannot attend the dinner in our ballroom." John never missed a beat. He replied, "I am making dinner arrangements for all of the people that I represent. If some of them are not welcome at your hotel, then I cannot have the dinner here." John's personal views never entered into the discussion. He was acting in a representative capacity and he refused to act against the interests of any of the letter carriers that he represented. He made dinner arrangements at a less "prestigious" location but one that catered to all of the members. Chalk up one for Brother Alfred's Sunday morning classes.

During the war, production of automobiles was stopped and manufacturing plants were devoted to the war effort. John was not particularly concerned about the shortage of cars. He had one of the best cars made, a 1936 Hudson Terraplane sedan. It was one of the first cars made with an automatic transmission. It also had a sleek, modern design. John loved that car. But when a strange man opened the passenger door while John was stopped for a red light on

Frankford Avenue, and pointed a pistol at him, John got out of the car without any hesitation. There was little that the police could do but look for the car and wait. Two weeks went by without any word. Finally, they found the car abandoned on a rural road in Bucks County. The thief had run it into the ground. All of the tires were flat. One of the tires looked like a spool of loose string. John could only wonder about the extent of the damage to the engine and the transmission. The insurance company treated it as a total loss. But very few cars were available as replacements. John decided to try to have the Hudson repaired. It was a bad decision. The car was never the same again.

    And John was learning that cars are not the only things that wear out. It was getting harder for John to finish his mail route each day. He had always suffered to some degree from rheumatism and arthritis but now there were extended bouts of phlebitis, and then hemorrhoid surgery. It was difficult to walk. John had been offered different post office jobs on several occasions. The next level at the post office was route examiner, which the carriers called "roundsman." The route examiner followed a letter carrier along his route and noted all of the things done wrong and the things that could be done better. Letter carriers *hated* roundsmen. John swore that he would never become one of those hated persons. But in 1948 he had no choice. His legs were giving out. John could no longer make deliveries and the only alternative was to become a route examiner. Grudgingly, he made the change.

    It wasn't long before John met his first real challenge. He was assigned to evaluate a letter carrier who had been constant trouble to everyone at his station. The station superintendent made it clear that he hoped the route examination would provide grounds for terminating this particular carrier. John was not comfortable with that situation. He was still a letter carrier at heart. He did not want to cause any letter carrier to lose his job. The day before the examination, he walked up next to the targeted carrier and, in a quiet voice said, "I am scheduled to examine your route tomorrow. Be on your toes." The carrier turned away, walked straight to the superintendent's office and reported John for disclosing confidential information. Fortunately for John, the superintendent was not terribly upset and the examination went forward as scheduled.

During the examination, it was obvious to John that the carrier saw him walking about a block behind. Nonetheless the results of the route inspection were awful. The examination provided exactly the kind of objective data needed to terminate the carrier. But John was uneasy. Something gnawed at him. If the carrier knew that he was being watched, why didn't he clean up his act? When he reached the conclusion part of his report, John wrote that in the absence of any explanation for the poor results recorded, he recommended that the carrier undergo a complete physical examination to determine whether there was a medical reason for the poor performance. His conclusion came straight out of his classes at La Salle. A physical examination was conducted and it disclosed that the carrier was suffering from a brain tumor. Medical treatment did not help the letter carrier, the tumor was too far developed. But everyone from the other carriers at the station all the way up to the postmaster heard of John's evaluation and they were impressed. Chalk up another one for Brother Alfred's labor-management school.

In his non-postal hours, John continued to support the political fortunes of his friends. One of the politically fortunate was Jim McGranery who, at the expiration of his term in congress had been appointed judge of the United States District Court for the Eastern District of Pennsylvania. He later gave up that position to become an assistant to the Attorney General of the United States under President Harry

S. Truman. In 1952, as his presidency was drawing to an end, Truman submitted to congress the name of James P. McGranery to fill the office of Attorney General of the United States.

The nomination was opposed by a prominent Philadelphia political figure, Richardson Dilworth, who attacked McGranery's character. John was furious but he was not surprised. Dilworth was impulsive. He often spoke his mind without considering either the truth or the consequences of what he was saying. In this case it was unlikely that Dilworth's remarks would have any influence on congress. But you could never tell about those things. Someone might believe Dilworth's charges. It might spark opposition. John spent every night for a week combing through old newspapers for stories about Dilworth criticizing other Philadelphia leaders. He found a lot of news articles of that type. He cut out the articles and put them in a scrapbook that he sent to a member of congress to demonstrate the lack of credibility of the man who had the gall to attack Jim McGranery. Congress approved the appointment.

John probably never heard of the maxim that "no good deed should go unpunished." However, almost immediately after McGranery took office, Brother Alfred contacted John suggesting rather strongly that the De La Salle Medal be presented to the Attorney General of the United States, James P. McGranery, before his short term in office ended in December 1952. Of course, John would handle the logistics. The dinner at the Bellevue-Stratford Hotel was a major undertaking. A featured speaker was General Walter Bedell Smith, Director of the Central Intelligence Agency. It was a great success but was also a lot of work. Since the dinner chairman spent most of the winter months in Florida, the work fell in John's lap. John was surprised the week after the dinner when he received a formal note from the "official chairman" thanking John for being of substantial assistance in helping Mr. Horan run a successful dinner. John was not used to this type of executive protocol and his first reaction was one of indignation. However, the reaction was only momentary. John did not have the time or the affluence to develop a grudge grounded on protocol.

Politicking came naturally to John. He was an effective communicator. He had energy, organizational experience and an articulate, persuasive manner. But he also had to deal with the Hatch Political Activity Act, which was usually referred to simply as "the Hatch Act." The Hatch Act was designed to work hand-in-glove with the civil service laws in preventing a successful political candidate from firing large numbers of government workers and giving their jobs to political supporters as had been the case under what was known as the "spoils system." The civil service laws provided an objective method of determining qualifications for government jobs and objective criteria for advancement. The Hatch Act made it a criminal offense for most federal employees to be directly involved in political activity. Although the law contained certain exceptions, such as those for heads of departments, it was generally applicable to letter carriers. The Hatch Act enjoyed partial success in achieving its objectives. Letter carriers were secure in their employment. On the other hand, everyone knew that the management positions in the post office went to those persons who had political influence. Thus, as a practical matter, the Hatch Act acted as a roadblock to letter carriers who wanted advancement. It was easier for outsiders to advance to the top jobs.

John avoided the cutting edge of the Hatch Act by pointing out that Betty was the member of the family who was politically active. The Hatch Act did not prohibit political activity by a spouse. And Betty was an active political worker. She was a committeewoman in the 35th

Ward and her responsibility was to cover the four-block precinct around their house. Betty was good at that job. She was a good listener and a good conversationalist. She went door-to-door and knew everyone by his or her first name. Republican party leaders in the 35th Ward viewed Betty as their biggest obstacle to carrying that precinct. On election days, Betty would spend long hours at the polls, trying to maintain an upbeat attitude even though she knew that the Democratic candidate faced certain defeat. In the meanwhile, John confined his activity to personal dealings with Byrne and Green and other party leaders and, of course, with the labor-management group from La Salle College.

With the 1952 election of Dwight D. Eisenhower as President of the United States, favored appointments in the post office began to go to a different group of people. One of the favored persons was George Harkins, a young clerk with whom John often worked in the Frankford Station. There was an age difference between them but George and John were friends and often joked about the political system that controlled their fortunes. Still, the Democratic Party enjoyed solid influence in local politics. It was a common occurrence for John's neighbors on Chippendale Avenue to seek his assistance in getting promotions or better work assignments in Philadelphia's police and fire departments. Some of them even indicated a willingness to pay for the favors but John would have none of that. Brother Alfred had taught him that it was dishonest for politicians to accept money from their constituents for doing what they had been elected to do. John was happy to be in a position to help his neighbors.

But John and Betty did have one serious problem with their neighbors. A few of the neighbors began to denigrate the two or three Jewish families who lived in the immediate neighborhood. It was as though they wanted to isolate those families and exclude them from the day-to-day neighborhood society. Betty was furious. She recalled her own experience as a teenager during the First World War when she was shunned by her North Philadelphia neighbors and called names because she had a German surname. She did not appreciate that experience and she did not want anyone else to endure that kind of thing. But John and Betty had to be careful how they handled the situation because their children knew the neighbors who were causing the problem and were friends of the children of those neighbors. In the end, they decided that they would not tell the children the details but they would talk generally about discrimination and about Betty's experiences when she was a child. Outside the house, they made it very clear to the neighbors that they did not support this type of exclusionary activity. Fortunately, the problem eventually dissipated and went away without further trouble.

Although Betty liked John's friend Walter Garvin, she did have mixed emotions about some of Garvin's friends. Garvin owned a neighborhood bar with the appropriate name "Garvin's Irishman." He was a slender man with a receding hairline. Walter would often call on John carrying a plain brown paper bag that invariably held a fifth of whiskey. "I thought that ye might like this," he would say, thrusting the package into John's hand. It was part of Walter Garvin's make-up that he did not want to call on a friend empty handed. Betty understood that. She was brought up the same way. She was uncomfortable with the fact that her paternal grandparents had separated but she always remembered that when old Boscilius Metzinger came to visit, he always had a gift for her grandmother, sometimes a drum of molasses, and other times a product from the Pennsylvania Dutch area of Bucks County where he had taken up residence. Betty liked that practice. And she also liked the lilting Irish brogue of Walter and his friends. "It sounds like music when they talk," she said. But she did not like it at all when their conversation turned to buying guns and ammunition to be sent back to the old country.

Betty also did not like the hours that John's friends kept. These men generally had their own businesses, usually real estate, insurance and tavern businesses. The political decisions were usually made at late night meetings at one of the taverns or at the Democratic Party's after hours social club. John generally structured his days around the schedule of politics. He would get home from work early in the afternoon and take a nap until dinnertime. In the early evening, he would go to John Byrne's taproom at 7412 Frankford Avenue and stay there until closing time. He would then get a few hours sleep before starting the next workday. Betty would attend the major social functions run by the political party but she was not a regular participant in the day-to-day social affairs of the party. She was a committeewoman and she acknowledged that politics got her the part time job as a receptionist at the State Highway Department, but Betty was not about to let politics replace her personal priorities, and she told that to John in no uncertain terms.

When Ray Thomas was appointed Postmaster of Philadelphia, John did not get the top promotions that Betty thought he deserved. Instead, Thomas appointed Tony Lambert to the key position. Lambert had started at the post office eight months *after* John. But John knew that Tony had also moved from letter carrier to a supervisory job in parcel post about a dozen years before John opted for the roundsman position. John had deliberately stayed with the letter carrier's job. In retrospect, Lambert had made a smart move. It broadened his background experience and made advancement more likely. John made it a point to seize every opportunity to fill in for post office managers who were on vacation or out due to illness. But in Betty's mind, it was simply that Ray Thomas had forgotten his friend John. As a general concept, Betty agreed with John's willingness to help others but when the persons he helped later found themselves in a position to help John, Betty expected those persons to reciprocate, even without being asked.

Betty's primary avocations were playing cards and playing bingo. Bridge was the favorite game at the card parties that would rotate from the home of one player to another on a regular basis. Betty had known Gert Helstab from her early childhood days in St. Edward's parish. Gert and her sister Margaret would often make a foursome with Betty and Margaret Carpinelli who lived directly across Chippendale Avenue. On most occasions, they would be joined by at least four other neighbors. On other nights, Betty and one or two of her friends would travel to one of three or four church halls where they played bingo. These games were attended on a regular schedule. Betty was a serious bingo player. She handled twenty or more cards at a time every evening.

By and large, John and Betty's interests came together on the critical issues confronting their family. During 1957, politics caused a crisis. John was never certain who was responsible but someone at the post office made an anonymous complaint against him. It was alleged that John had engaged in political activity in violation of the Hatch Act. It may have been a result of the dinner that he organized in honor of Pennsylvania's Democratic Governor George Leader. An investigation was conducted by the United States Civil Service Commission. A violation could result in the loss of his job and a forfeiture of more than thirty years of hard work. The investigator interviewed personnel at the post office and even checked John's attendance records to determine whether he had spent an inordinate amount of time away from the job. Absences might support a charge that he was working on political rather than postal business much of the time. John knew that the investigation was taking place and he knew that he had to be extremely careful. It was a constant subject of discussion between John and Betty. The children were warned to be careful about talking to unidentified callers on the phone. Finally, on December 10, 1957, John was advised that the investigation failed to substantiate the allegations and that the commission's file was being closed.

John continued to receive long handwritten letters from Brother Alfred and Brother Al continued to urge that the De La Salle Medal be presented to President Dwight D. Eisenhower. John followed up and even arranged for the medal to be struck. It was a handsome, heavy medal in a velvet-lined box. John kept it in the desk in his living room. But John had little affection for Dwight Eisenhower.

John just could not picture himself presenting the De La Salle Medal to Ike the way he had presented it to Roosevelt. And most of John's friends felt the same way. So they continued to drag their feet and the medal remained in the box, in the drawer, in the desk in John's living room. Finally, the issue was resolved in 1957 when John received a phone call informing him that Brother Alfred had died. The box stayed in the desk drawer until eight years later when Brother Thomas J. Donaghy and Brother Patrick Ellis came to Chippendale Avenue to interview John as part of Brother Thomas' research for his book *"Conceived in Crisis: A History of La Salle College."* John gave them the medal for La Salle's archives.

The passing of Brother Alfred reminded John of his mentor's emphasis on education and stirred within an uneasy feeling that he was losing control of his ability to chart the educational paths of his children. Young Jack had graduated from the University of Pennsylvania and was in the navy, serving aboard the aircraft carrier, USS Forrestal. The scholarship that he won from the navy paid for his college education and was a big financial boost to the family. Gerard was struggling through St. Joe's but seemed more interested in ball games and his friends than he was in studying. John smiled as he recalled entering the Democratic Club at the Poquessing Golf Course and seeing Gerard seated at the bar talking to Rosemary and Norman Payne. John positioned himself on the other side of the room in plain view of anyone seated at the bar. After a few minutes, he looked back over to the bar. It was empty except for Rosemary and Norman. "When does he study?" John worried. John could understand the time spent at the Democratic Club. It was the time wasted at ball games that he could not figure out.

John was at a complete loss when it came to dealing with his daughter. In the 1950's it was not a particularly common thing for the daughters of government workers to attend college but both John and Betty wanted that for their daughter. Yet, the harder John tried, the less he succeeded. Pat dropped out of high school and took a job. John pictured himself walking out of eighth grade. It was *deja vu* all over again. He made a big mistake those many years ago. It would be an even bigger mistake for his daughter to drop out now. So, he lost his temper and insisted and demanded — and each harsh word became a fresh mistake. Privately, he blamed himself. He had not been able to describe the value of education as Brother Alfred had described it to him. John had communicated the value of education much in the same ineffective fashion that his father had told him about the dangers of icebergs in the north Atlantic. Maybe he should have done something different. But what?

Betty felt much the same as John, but she handled it differently. When she was young, Betty had also wanted to follow her own star. She left home at an early age. She lived for a while with her friends, the Helstabs. She rented a room. Betty was not there when her mother got sick and died of the flu. Betty developed a firm, long-range outlook. She focused on the long-term goal and was satisfied with any development that moved, however slightly, in that direction. Betty was a plodder, a survivor.

In the meanwhile, the Frankford Post Office Station, which had been the largest substation in the nation, was divided and one part of it was designated as a new post office named Boulevard Station. George Harkins was named as superintendent. John was appointed assistant superintendent. The building was unique in that it shared a wedge-shaped parcel of land between Levick Street and Harbison Avenue with a municipal building that was used as a district headquarters for the Philadelphia Police Department. Although the federal and the municipal functions of the buildings were quite different, the men in charge of the two facilities had frequent contact with one another to coordinate their mutual problems. John and George Harkins got along quite well with their counterpart from the police department. In fact, John developed a genuine respect for the outspoken Captain Frank L. Rizzo. He thought that Rizzo more than made up for his lack of education by the exercise of good judgment and common sense.

Not long before Boulevard Station opened, John Byrne and his brother Joe bought the old Cottage Green Inn on Ashton Road near Holme Circle. The "Blue Laws" were still in effect and bars were subject to early closing hours and Sunday sales were prohibited. However, a new law would provide an exception for hotels and inns that rented out rooms. The Cottage qualified under the exception because it had two or three rooms, even though, as a practical matter, they were never rented out. One room was a permanent home for Buck Ryan, a Wallace Beery look-alike carpenter who had an affection for alcohol and who worked full time for the Byrnes. The other rooms just stayed vacant. Their only function was to qualify the Cottage for Sunday sales. Cottage Green quickly became the headquarters for Byrne's political operations. And John made the Cottage his own base of operations, often volunteering to act as the restaurant's maître d'.

It was with mixed emotions one evening that John told the Byrne brothers that his youngest son had enlisted in the Marines. He would report to Quantico in September. There was a twinge of envy. John enjoyed his own experience in the Marines, including an exercise at Quantico. And he was proud and just a little bit jealous of his youngest brother, Bill, who had been a Marine during the war. But how could anyone who was incapable of following his father's clear directions at home ever hope to survive the demands of the Marine Corps? "He's in for a rude awakening," John predicted. Byrne just smiled. Byrne often told his own sons that they should be more like John St. John's boys. In all probability, John Byrne mentioned the Marine Corps to young John and Neil the next day.

John had experienced a rude shock the previous year when he stopped to say hello to his mother. Her mind had slipped badly. John no longer saw his mother with the frequency that prevailed a dozen or so years earlier. Holiday dinners no longer included the extended family. The children were older now and some holidays, such as Christmas and Easter, no longer had the same meaning to them. The children also resisted large family gatherings that impinged on their own social lives. Betty too was not particularly enthusiastic about crowding all those people into one row house. Little by little, the time between John's visits to his mother grew longer and longer.

Liz St. John was one of those persons whose appearance never seemed to change. She still looked the same. But John noticed immediately that something was different. There was a slowness of mind, an air of indifference to her family. She had trouble remembering things and remembering people. The doctors said that it was nothing to be concerned about, that she was just growing old. On one occasion, she did not even recognize John. It was as though she was a completely different person, an elderly lady who looked and sounded just like his mother but thought and acted differently. Years ago, his father had suffered excruciating pain but he never lost his mind. Right up to the end, Charlie St. John made his own decisions. Maybe there were some things worse than physical pain. Liz St. John died on June 11, 1959. She was 80 years of age. John silently prayed that he would never lose his mind.

Happy Days Are Here Again

As 1960 approached, it seemed as though political fortunes were shifting and that the Democrats might regain their presidential momentum. John heard about the overtures that were being made to Bill Green and others by Joe Kennedy on behalf of Kennedy's son John who was then a Senator from Massachusetts. John did not like what he heard. It was one thing to win an election. It was another thing to buy it. On the other hand, John could sense the enthusiasm that was building among younger voters who supported the youthful senator from Massachusetts. It was the type of enthusiasm that the established party candidate, Adlai Stevenson, could not muster. Joe Kennedy just might pull it off. But John would not concern himself with the presidential race. Bill Green was taking the lead in whipping up support for the presidential candidate. John was content to work behind the scenes assisting John Byrne in the local elections.

John was surprised by the election results. He was not surprised that Kennedy won Philadelphia by a landslide. John had worked more than twenty years to build that effective political organization. But he was surprised that Kennedy won the national election, and he was surprised at the closeness of the race. Closer to home, he was glad that Bill Green emerged from the election with a great deal of influence in the new administration. And he proudly displayed in his living room the bronze medal that John Byrne brought back for him from Kennedy's inauguration. But he still felt that Joe Kennedy bought the election and, maybe he even bought Bill Green.

John also knew that the political stars were aligned as never before. He mentioned to John Byrne that the Postmaster of Philadelphia, Anthony Lambert, was about to retire and that John St. John would very much like to be the next Postmaster. He had 36 years of experience in the post office and had handled virtually every aspect of the postal service at one time or another. John also knew that he would have the support of career post office people. It was the first time in their long acquaintance that John had asked for anything for himself. Byrne took it up with Bill Green. Green said that it was a good idea. Green would submit John's name to President Kennedy for appointment. In the meanwhile, it was arranged for John to receive an interim appointment as "Acting Assistant Postmaster of Philadelphia."

The Postmaster's position was now vacant. For all practical purposes, John was doing the job of the Postmaster. It would just be a matter of time. But John underestimated the level of avarice and self-interest inherent in the political process. Other people wanted the job of Postmaster, not because of any postal experience but because they felt that they were entitled to it by reason of the political favors that they had done for one politician or another. Someone suggested that John did not have the education for the job. They said that he not only did not have a college degree but that he really had not attended high school; that he just took a general equivalency test. And then came the announcement from Washington. Someone else was appointed Postmaster of Philadelphia.

Bill Green swore that he had nothing to do with the snub. He said that he too was a victim; that another Philadelphian had given the other name to Kennedy's people and that Kennedy acted on it with the understanding that this was the person who had Philadelphia's backing. Green said that the very next day he directed all of the congressmen from Philadelphia to cast their votes against a bill proposed by the Kennedy Administration and, when asked the reason, to say that they had been directed to do so by Green. Later that same day, Green said that a Kennedy aide called on him and inquired about Philadelphia's vote. Green asked the aide if he had contacted the other congressmen from Philadelphia. He had. Each said that he had been directed how to vote by Bill Green. The aide asked why Green had given that order. Green answered the question with a question. Did the Kennedy Administration now know who spoke for Philadelphia's congressional delegation? If so, there would be no problem in the future.

The next week, Congressman Green submitted John's name for appointment to the position of Director of Personnel for the Eastern Region of the United States Post Office. Again questions were raised about John's educational qualifications, this time directly by the post office staff who reviewed the proposed appointment. Someone else wanted that job too. Again there was a delay. But Bill Green followed up this time and John took office in December 1961.

The director of personnel did not have the high public profile of the Postmaster of Philadelphia, but the eastern region was a much larger geographic area, covering Pennsylvania, New Jersey and Delaware. The director's job included presiding at the swearing-in ceremonies for the postmasters in all of the communities in the region. Typically, the new postmasters were political appointees and were persons of great influence in those communities. The installation ceremonies were covered in the local newspapers and were accompanied by receptions in the town halls. John enjoyed the ceremonies and the people who attended them. In turn, the community leaders and media were greatly impressed by the distinguished appearance, public speaking skills and long postal experience of the "big shot" from Philadelphia. John would usually drive to the ceremony. Although he was often unfamiliar with the surroundings, he knew that it was easy to find the post office. "You just look for the building with the American flag out front," he would say.

    In Ridgewood, New Jersey, the newly installed postmaster was an influential member of the Republican Party. He feigned surprise when John presented him with a large, framed photograph of President John F. Kennedy to be hung in the post office. John smiled at the new postmaster and said that he wanted to have the photo autographed but that was done only "in election years." Everyone laughed. Photographers snapped pictures for the next day's newspaper. And then they all repaired to the firehouse hall for a celebration. John topped off the day

John St. John (Feb. 1963) N. Bergen, NJ

by stopping in to see his brother Reds who lived in North Bergen, just outside New York City.

The regional director of personnel was also the official who would make arrangements for educational seminars to be presented by members of the faculty at major universities for the benefit of the postal managers. John particularly enjoyed the classes on time management and on decision-making. The seminars would be a big help to the next level of management as they advanced toward the top jobs in the post office. In effect, he was continuing the work of Brother Alfred. And since it was strictly an administrative office, John could set his own hours and avoid the rush hour traffic on the Schuylkill Expressway. It gradually dawned on John that this was a far better job than being Postmaster of Philadelphia.

John knew that political opportunity was a fickle thing. It would be hard to improve on the present circumstance in which John Byrne practically ran the Democratic Party's City Committee and Bill Green had the ear of the President of the United States. Such enhanced political clout certainly had not hurt the real estate and insurance businesses of Byrne and Green, and Green also stood to make a fortune on the new Liberty Bell Race Track that was opening in the northeast part of the city. Important political figures always seemed to know what development opportunities were materializing and were usually in a position to share in the profits. And now the federal government was making millions of dollars available for redevelopment and other social projects. John suggested to his friends at Cottage Green Inn that they form a holding company to develop government-funded projects. In effect, they could use federal funds with very little risk and achieve major profits. It was a model being followed by entrepreneurs throughout the country. It was a very good idea. Investing a few thousand dollars each, they created the Northeast Holding Corporation.

It was a learning experience. Powerful political connections were not enough. A number of other skills were also needed. Someone had to be able to evaluate the enterprise and determine whether it could be built within the available time and cost parameters. Someone had to develop the building plans, including the sequence of contractors needed to complete the job. And someone had to oversee the construction from beginning to end. The Northeast Holding group did not have those skills. They were all "little guys." They did not know where to begin. Then, one member of the group seized an opportunity. He pointed out that the company's money was just sitting in a bank and not earning any money. He proposed using the money for mortgages which would be a safe investment until a development opportunity presented itself. In effect, he used the holding company as a private bank to support his own marginal real estate sales. Within a very short time, the holding company's funds were totally committed to mortgages on undesirable real estate in deteriorating neighborhoods. John tried to halt the skid but he did not have the necessary skills either. Opportunity passed them by.

Not a Leg to Stand on

While the Northeast Holding Corporation foundered, John found himself preoccupied with a more serious concern. He was wearing out. His legs were getting increasingly weaker. A few years earlier, after what was supposed to have been a routine hernia operation, he noticed a weakness in his legs. At the time, he thought that it was just another side effect of the cigarettes that he smoked almost continuously. But then he passed out for a few seconds while driving home on the expressway. He was not tired or sleepy. But one minute he was wide awake and the next minute he was not.

When consciousness returned, he was in the same lane of traffic and the cars around him were in the same relative positions. He pulled over to the side of the road and rested for a while before continuing home. Then it happened again at home. He mentioned it to his friend "Doc" Callaghan. Joseph J. Callaghan was a medical doctor who worked for the state. He was the only medical person that John trusted. Years ago, John felt the same way about Vernon G. Nickelson but "Dr. Nick" had long since passed away.

Doc Callaghan made arrangements for some tests. He did not seem surprised by the results. He told John that it looked like a vascular problem. There was very little circulation in his legs, and that was just the start. Other complications were likely. Doc recommended that John go on medical disability and then submit to a complete battery of tests at the Hospital of the University of Pennsylvania. John filed for disability in February 1963 and left the job in the middle of March. In early September, he was admitted to the hospital for testing.

The doctors at Penn found several serious problems. There was infiltrate on the right lung, almost certainly a tumor. Between March, when the first x-rays were taken, and September, it had more than doubled in size. Given John's history of cigarette smoking, the prognosis for the lung was not good. The circulation in his left leg was almost completely blocked. The doctors warned that an injury to the legs, even a severe bruise, could result in an amputation or, maybe two amputations. Even under the best of circumstances, there was very little that the doctors could do for that degree of blockage. The prostate was enlarged and might require surgery. Finally, there were questions as to the health of John's heart. Each of these conditions was serious. Taken together, they were a disaster.

The doctors suggested that the lung be addressed first. If that could be successfully treated, they would then consider the circulatory problem. While John was in the hospital, a patient assigned to the same room was diagnosed with a similar lung condition. When the condition was explained to him, the man lay back on his bed, crying compulsively. He continued to cry through the rest of the day. John asked the hospital staff if he could be transferred to another room so that he could think clearly. Then he went about making arrangements for his own surgery. He insisted on an interim discharge from the hospital. In late September, he would attend his oldest son's wedding in Monterrey, Mexico where young Jack was a Foreign Service officer in the United States Consulate. Afterward, John would check back into the hospital. Although the doctors advised against any delay in the surgery, they went along with John's plan.

Both John and Joe Byrne knew the seriousness of John's medical condition. They knew about the surgery and they knew about the wedding in Mexico. They suspected that the lung problem was cancer. The Byrnes decided that they would join John on the trip to Monterrey. Another Cottage Green "regular," Jack McGinley, said that he would go too. They were afraid that John would not last long after the lung operation and they knew that this might be their last time together. Picking up on Edwin O'Connor's *"The Last Hurrah,"* the best selling novel modeled after Boston's Mayor James Michael Curley, they called their trip *"The Last Olé."*

It had been a long time since John had a vacation or had traveled anywhere with his closest friends or his family. John, his family and friends made up for lost time. They celebrated in private homes in Monterrey. They celebrated at a nearby country club. They celebrated in Monterrey's restaurants. And they even had an afternoon "Fishtown Party," a throwback to the old days at the Tin Brick. The Fishtown Party brought Joe Byrne's day to an abrupt halt in mid-afternoon. It even put a serious dent in his activities the following morning. The wedding almost took a

The Last Ole' :
John St. John, Joe Bryne, John F. Bryne and Jack McGinley
Monterrey, Mexico, September 1963.

back seat to the wedding celebrations. It ended too soon. John returned to Philadelphia and checked back into the hospital. The operation took place on October 9, 1963.

Had he known what the operation would be like, John said that he would never have gone through with it. He would have let the disease run its course. The surgeons made a very long incision down his side near the arm; a rib was broken and pulled back out of the way; and then began the removal of the lung. It was a difficult procedure. John was awakened in the recovery room. Something had gone wrong. There was continued bleeding in the lung cavity. Would he consent to going back into the operating room for another attempt at closing the bleeding? Were they kidding? Did he have any choice? When the operation was completed, he looked like he was dead, and felt worse.

It was a day or two before he could focus well enough to carry on a conversation with the doctors and visitors. They brought him into a conference room where the team of surgeons tried to explain the details of the operation. It was highly technical and difficult to understand. They did not use the word "cancer" but you could almost feel it in the muggy atmosphere of the room. They said that there was only a five percent statistical probability of living beyond five years and that they were unable to predict mortality within that five-year period. That was when John reached into his shirt pocket, took out a cigarette and lighted it. The chief surgeon started to admonish him but then thought better of it, saying simply, "I wish that you wouldn't do that." John knew that he was showing off but he had gone this far and there was no way that he was going to put out that cigarette. Who were they kidding? You don't qualify for statistics like that just because it was a tough operation. The cigarette was his sign of protest.

Given his poor prognosis, an operation on the vascular system was out of the question. John was discharged to his home. He could barely get upstairs to the second floor bedroom. Everything hurt. He was too weak to get out of bed. Soon John noticed that his skin was getting dark. It looked like he had a suntan. He joked with visitors about spending too much time at the beach. But he had developed hepatitis from the blood transfusions he received during surgery. Gradually, some of his strength returned but he felt awful.

In November, John pushed himself to get dressed and get out of the house. He decided to join his friends at Cottage Green. Appearances were deceiving. John looked healthier than many of his friends. But it was disconcerting the way that they hovered near him, as if to be in a position to catch him if he fell. At one point, John did stumble on an irregularity in the floor -- and three men leaped from nearby tables with their arms outstretched to break his fall. After about two hours, John called it a night and asked his son to drive him home. John's friends breathed a collective sigh of relief. Now they could have a drink and relax.

The recovery was painfully slow. John limited his activities around the house. Most evenings he would drive to the Cottage for an hour or two. But his full strength was not returning. He longed to get back to the post office but he knew that was not in the cards. Even if a medical miracle occurred, things had changed. The three men who brought about his appointment to the eastern region, John Byrne, Bill Green and President Kennedy, were all dead. Kennedy was assassinated in November 1963; Bill Green died of a brain tumor about a month later; and John Byrne suffered a fatal heart attack the following year. John Byrne's brother Joe was not far behind. He too had a brain tumor. The trip to Mexico had been *The Last Olé* after all.

Despite his illness, John spearheaded an effort that resulted in city-owned Poquessing Golf Course being renamed in memory of John F. Byrne. He also served as co-chairman of a fundraising drive that resulted in the John F. Byrne scholarship being created at La Salle College. At first, John tried to downplay the scholarship effort. He was not sure that they would be able to raise sufficient funds and he was afraid that the fundraising effort might dampen the political support that he knew would be there for the memorial renaming of the golf course. As it turned out, both efforts were successful. The political support remained firm and the renaming was approved by City Council. The fundraising drive raised more than $17,000.00, which was sufficient to support the John F. Byrne Scholarship. A short dedication ceremony was held at the golf course in July 1966. Mayor James H. J. Tate presided. There were five speakers on the program. Everyone in attendance agreed that John was by far the best speaker at the ceremony.

Any surge of energy that John might have experienced in establishing the Byrne memorials was offset by his latest medical evaluation. The doctors at HUP confirmed that there were no new tumors but traces of the disease that they did not want to talk about were in the vascular system. They recommended that any further surgery be deferred unless there was an emergency. John didn't complain. But he was weak. Arthritis made his shoulders ache. He was spending more time in bed. When he did go downstairs, he would sit on the steps and negotiate them one step at a time. During the Easter holidays, Betty became ill. Her stomach was upset and it seemed as though everything ached. She just wanted to lie down and rest. After several days without improvement, she went to the hospital and was admitted immediately. It was a heart attack. At home, John pushed himself to get out of bed, cook his own meals and generally do the things around the house that Betty had been doing. The activity seemed to bring back some of his strength. On the other hand, it may have been the result of his new medication. The doctors had prescribed two shots of whiskey each day for his vascular condition.

The long inactive days gave John plenty of time to think. It reaffirmed his longstanding belief that the employment benefits of the post office were far superior to those of private businesses. His medical care was guaranteed by the government and he had elected that his pension be transferred to Betty in the event of his death. Not every pension plan offered that option. And many private pension plans did not survive the financial failure of the underlying business. John was glad that he did not leave the post office to join Bill Green back in 1945. The post office had been a solid employer. But John was not content to sit at home and collect the federal benefits that he had earned. John wanted to get back into the action. He knew important people. He would get back into the fray, either in the post office or in politics.

At first, John did not notice his memory slip. He called Pat Carr to discuss an aspect of the Northeast Holding Corporation. John still held the office of president. He had barely raised the subject at hand when Carr said, "But John, we discussed that point this morning. Don't you remember?" John did not remember. But he mumbled, "Oh yes, of course we did. It just slipped my mind in the press of other things that I have been doing." John then cut the conversation short and hung up the phone. He was alarmed. That had never happened before. There was no reason for him to forget a telephone conversation that occurred just an hour or two earlier. And then it happened again, and again. It was getting worse. Was this the way it started with Mom?

Joshua Eilberg, who had recently been elected to congress, called on John and asked him to work on Eilberg's staff. The congressman needed someone with experience and credibility to deal with potential contributors. John liked Josh Eilberg and wanted to help him. It was the kind of activity he had been searching for. John agreed to join the staff. But the deteriorating memory quickly got in the way. John had to tell Eilberg that he could not continue. John was now reluctant to call anyone on the phone. He was afraid that he might have just finished talking to them and would be embarrassed by his forgetfulness. John's world was getting smaller.

There were emergency admissions to the hospital, sometimes for pneumonia but most of them heart related. Doc Callaghan thought that they were cerebral accidents, the things that people often call "mini-strokes." One evening, John was certain that one of these events would be final. He could accept that. It was plain that the medical profession could not restore his health, that he was on a steady downward progression. When John lost consciousness, Betty called the emergency squad. The firemen were quick and efficient. They hurried upstairs and set up a stretcher. Just then, John awakened and ordered them out of the house. He had no intention of going to the hospital. Doc Callaghan tried to reason with John but without success. "I can't just sit here and watch this," said Doc, and he went down to the kitchen, poured himself a bourbon and sat down to wait it out. Upstairs, John was slipping in and out of consciousness. One thought began to bother him. Suppose that this attack was not fatal. Suppose that it left him partially impaired for lack of medical treatment. "Maybe you had better call back that rescue squad," he said.

John spent about a week in Nazareth Hospital. Most evenings at about 9:30, well after the end of visiting hours, the nurses on duty would see a slender, balding man with a brown paper bag tucked under his arm walk out of the stairwell and into John's room. Ten minutes later they would see him leave without the paper bag. They wondered, but they never discovered what he had been carrying. John always hid the bottle in the drawer next to his bed until someone could take it home.

One night on the way home from the Cottage, John's attention was diverted to the other side of the street and the wreckage of an accident that occurred earlier in the evening. John did not notice that the car in front of him put on the brakes to get a better look at that same accident. The rear end accident that resulted was a minor thing but it caused a great deal of aggravation. John had just dropped his own automobile insurance coverage in protest against the high rates. The increasing insurance premiums seemed to be a waste of money considering his safe driving record. The other motorist brought suit and John had to retain a lawyer in Josh Eilberg's firm to represent him. The suit was resolved but it took about a year and the settlement payment plus the lawyer's fees far exceeded the insurance premium that John had "saved." Now, he rarely attempted to drive. Yet, he did not want to sell the car. That would be an admission that he would not recover. It was not his nature to give up hope. The car sat parked at the curb in front of the house. It was like a monument to the past and the way that things once were. But things were changing.

Even the neighborhood had changed. Chippendale Avenue was no longer the last block in northeast Philadelphia. Far from it. Houses now covered the entire three and one-half miles from Chippendale Avenue north to the Bucks County line. John Byrne's nephew Jimmy owned the Cottage Green. Although Jimmy treated John as a member of the family, it was not the same at the Cottage without John and Joe Byrne. And John's only contact with the post office was the annual dinner of the postmasters association, which he was able to attend through the good will of Andy Derham who worked in the eastern region and had come to admire John. Derham was not permitted to attend those dinners. He was not a member of the postmasters association. He was just a postal employee, but a loyal one. He would drop off John at the dinner and then drive around for a while, or stop for coffee. After about three hours, Derham would pick up John and drive him home. At the dinners, the master of ceremonies often announced that John was one of the few persons who held membership in both the postmasters association and the National Association of Letter Carriers. The announcement usually drew spontaneous applause from the crowd. In John's mind, that was not anything to cheer about. It only showed how effective the Hatch Act had been at limiting the advancement of letter carriers.

The children were now raising families of their own. John hoped for their success but he dared not interfere with them at this stage of their lives. He was settling in to the role of patriarch of the family. John could not figure out exactly how it had happened but both of his sons not only graduated from college but went on to further education; Jack at Princeton and Ger at Temple's law school. They had done that on their own. Now, for the most part, John's attention was focused on his first grandson, Pat's boy, Jerry. The two spent a great deal of time together. John enjoyed talking to the youngster and watching his progress. Maybe John could help Jerry learn some of the things he would need to know later in life. A special bond developed between the grandfather and grandson.

In the meanwhile, visitors to the house on Chippendale Avenue would notice the mail that came from religious organizations. In particular there were the tracts published by the Christophers. John had not been far from these subjects all along but now they were on the kitchen table. He and Betty discussed the topics covered in the pamphlets. They also discussed them with the parish priests and the hospital chaplains. John had come full circle.

John beat the statistical probabilities that were explained to him at the hospital. He beat them almost by double. He lasted nine hard years battling cancer, vascular disease, hepatitis, memory loss and fatigue. He did it without complaint, adjusting to each new setback as it occurred. Deteriorating health became a common enemy for John and Betty. They drew strength from each other. John was finally ground down by a series of strokes on December 28, 1972. He was 68 years old. For the most part, he escaped the devastating effects of Alzheimer's disease. Delusions set in during the last two hospitalizations but that was about the extent of it other than the short-term memory loss. When the end came, his insurance and pension papers were found together in a neat file folder, with specific instructions written in longhand on index cards that were clipped to the appropriate papers. A day or two after John died; George Harkins came to Chippendale Avenue, sat down at the dining room table, and completed all of the annuity forms for transferring John's pension to Betty.

Betty was content to let the children handle the funeral arrangements. They selected a gravesite in the recently opened Resurrection Cemetery on Hulmeville Road. It was in a newly-opened section of the cemetery dedicated to St. Joseph the Worker. In May 1955, about a dozen years after Cardinal Dougherty shut down Brother Alfred's labor-management school, Pope Pius XII instituted the feast of St. Joseph the Worker. It was intended as an incentive to all those involved in the enterprise of labor to devote themselves to the realization of a social order in keeping with the Gospel. It would be hard to find a more appropriate burial site than one dedicated to the principles of industrial peace that were at the heart of Brother Alfred's work.

At the funeral Mass at St. Matthew's Church, the homilist, an eloquent priest who had not known John, glanced at the obituary and made an assumption that he did not bother to verify. He spoke of John and Betty's nine enjoyable years of retirement. The priest's mistake was lost on most of the congregation who were mainly friends of John and Betty's children and who had not known John well. Most of John's close friends had died before him. But seated quietly in the last pew of the church was Ray Thomas. He knew.

Betty's heart grew weaker and she stayed closer to home. Bingo was a thing of the past. Betty shared John's dislike of the medical profession. Plagued by gall bladder problems for years, she tried to cope with it by watching her diet rather than seeking medical care and risking surgery. When it came to dental problems, she would rather have a tooth extracted and be done with it. Now Betty was finding that those approaches came back to haunt her with a vengeance in her later years. Her energy waned. She noticed that even her childhood friends were becoming difficult to endure. "I would like to see Gert, but all she talks about any more is her latest operation and how bad she feels. I don't need that," said Betty, "I already feel bad."

Betty was spending most of her time near the old black and white television set. Her eyes were not comfortable with the light emitted by color television. Unlike John, Betty had been influenced by the athletic interests of their sons. She now followed Philadelphia's professional teams. On one occasion when asked how she planned to spend the evening, Betty's response was, "Well, I had planned to watch the Sixers' game against New York but Billy Cunningham just had surgery on his knee and Willis Reed is out with a hip pointer, so what kind of game can that be?" She was more than just a casual sports fan.

One snowy evening in 1976, Betty was half-sitting, half-lying on the living room sofa. She did not feel right. She could not make herself comfortable. Betty lost her balance and rolled onto the floor. She couldn't pull herself back up. Her words were thick and jumbled. She was suffering a stroke. The emergency squad rushed her to Nazareth Hospital. Betty recovered. The movement and the speech returned but the stroke destroyed her initiative. It was almost impossible to work up the incentive to practice the very basic movements that her physical condition required. Betty decided to sell the house on Chippendale Avenue and move in with her daughter in Southampton. The Chippendale Avenue property sold for a price of $31,500.00, about six times the original purchase price. It had been the family home for 37 years.

Betty's heart continued to weaken. She suffered repeated attacks of congestive heart failure. It became an all too familiar routine; the accumulation of fluid in the lungs, the frightening feeling of suffocation, the emergency race to the hospital, the drainage procedure, and then it would start all over again. In late October 1977, she was admitted to Holy Redeemer Hospital for the fifth time in as many months. Betty was exhausted. She knew that she could not last much longer, and she no longer cared. Betty's heart finally gave out during the afternoon of October 27, 1977, at the age of 78 years.

Epilogue

Well, that is how it would look if I tried to write in an impersonal style. A few difficult and emotional factors were omitted, as were some intra family piques and a large number of isolated occurrences involving persons and events not central to the theme. The omissions were strictly judgment calls on my part. One suspects that the omissions do not make a significant difference in the narrative.

The narrative took a jumble of nostalgic memories and forged them together in a more or less chronological sequence with facts that are recorded in letters, files and other writings. The effort just may have achieved the intended goal.

It reminds me of a song, *"Johnny I hardly knew ye!"*

THE KAISER ON THE CORNER

We lived in the fourth house from the corner. Looking from our back bedroom window to the right and across the driveway, I had a good view of the corner house at 3401 Oakmont Street. That corner property was owned by Robert C. Boger, a fiftyish, heavy-set man who doted on his lawn and the flowers in his garden. Instinctively, all of the neighborhood children knew that we should not set foot on Mr. Boger's lawn – at least when he was in the immediate area. We also knew that if he was a dozen or so yards away, that admonition could be safely ignored because we could easily outrun him. For his part, Bob Boger kept track of those incidents and inferred from them a God-given authority to drench any prior transgressor who happened to pass by while Bob was watering his lawn.

After dinner, when his garden hose was safely stored in the garage, Bob and Elizabeth Boger would sit in wicker chairs by their sidewalk on Crispin Street, talking to passers-by. Actually, it would be Bob who talked to them. Bob generally wore khaki work trousers and an old white T-shirt. He looked like he needed a shave. In contrast, Elizabeth was prim and proper, and looked for all the world like the Sunday school teacher that she once was. In some ways, Bob and Elizabeth were the odd couple. Nonetheless, they projected an appearance of being comfortable, care-free, and well-to-do. Appearances can be deceiving.

Bob Boger's family owned a textile manufacturing business with properties in Philadelphia and Charlotte, North Carolina. Commuters on Philadelphia's Market-Frankford Elevated trains could not help but notice the name "Boger & Crawford" on a large smokestack just west of the Tioga Street Station. Most people did not realize it at the time but Philadelphia's textile business was slowly drying up. Bob was well aware that textile work was going south and that it soon would be going to third-world countries in the Far East. The world had changed since the early 1900s when his father started the business.

Bob viewed his father with mixed emotions. He liked his father's strong German heritage. Also, he was proud of his father's genius for business and his role in the establishment of the Philadelphia College of Textiles and Science, which has since evolved into the present-day Philadelphia University. Each year, Philadelphia Textile would present the Robert C. Boger, Sr. Award for proficiency in power weaving.

Bob proudly recalled that his father "could walk down the city streets for miles, bantering with people as he went – and then tell you exactly how many people he passed, how many were carrying packages, how many were empty-handed, how many were men and how many were women." He would then put those observations to good use in his business dealings.

The elder Boger's analytical mind also guided his dealings with the textile labor force. In the 1920s, he had a very practical approach to labor relations. Like the workers in most of the textile businesses in Kensington, Boger & Crawford's workers lived in nearby rowhouses. A substantial number of the workers were Catholic and, accordingly, members of Ascension Parish, at G and Westmoreland Streets. Boger knew that donations to the Ladies' Auxiliary of Ascension Parish would do wonders in motivating the women of the parish to make sure that their husbands showed up for work on Monday mornings, regardless of how much they drank over the weekend. Similarly, the purchase of baseball bats, balls and uniforms for the Ascension CYO teams was not only a good civic gesture; it was a good labor relations expense.

Perhaps the best remembered of those labor expenses was incurred on Tuesday, September 4, 1923. Early that evening, the Ascension baseball team played a fundraising game against an all-star team sponsored by Lit Brothers department store. Playing first base for Ascension was Babe Ruth, who had just completed an afternoon game in which his New York Yankees defeated the Philadelphia Athletics at Shibe Park. More than 10,000 fans showed up to watch the Babe at I and Tioga Streets, where the baseball diamond was named "Boger Field." It is not clear whether Bob Boger's father had a hand in arranging for Babe Ruth to play that evening, but the name of the ball field suggests that he had something to do with it. In the meanwhile, residents of Kensington and the surrounding neighborhoods talked about that game for the rest of their lives.

Babe Ruth, playing for Ascension CYO at Boger Field, I and Tioga Streets, Philadelphia, Pa., September 4, 1923.

In contrast to his business success, Bob Boger's father was a self-destructive alcoholic. Bob talked about that side of his father years later when I was practicing law. He never forgot how his father regularly failed to come home for dinner. Rather than feeding the rest of the family at the normal dinner hour, Bob's mother would insist that all of them "wait until your father comes home" before anyone

89

could eat. The Bogers' irregular lifestyle threw Bob into turmoil. Given Bob's independent streak and outspoken nature, it is likely that he confronted his mother and challenged the way that she catered to the father's problem drinking. Maybe that is why his mother disliked Bob.

I thought that Mr. Boger was joking when he said that his mother did not like him; but he was dead serious. After Bob's father died, his mother decided to cut Bob out of her will. She told him that she was leaving everything to Bob's brother Ernie and his sister. She told the family lawyer to draw up a provision for a trust that would provide income for those two children and, after their death, the remaining assets would go to their children. Fortunately for Bob Boger, the lawyer drafted the trust fund for the benefit of all three children. When Fredericka complained that was not what she wanted, "The old Teuton told her 'Dot is die vay ve do it!' "Sign the will!" She did as she was told. Apparently, old German women did not argue with their lawyers in those days.

Bob Boger told me that story when he asked me to write his will. One of the terms he insisted on was that there would be no trust fund in his will. Bob had learned from practical experience with his mother's trust fund. He hated trusts.

Fredericka Boger's trust was handled by a prominent Philadelphia bank. Bob was not surprised that the bankers had no expertise in the textile business. However, that type of business expertise was exactly what was needed in an industry that was rapidly declining. Only the most aggressive and innovative textile businesses survived. The bank was neither aggressive nor innovative. Eventually, the plant near Tioga Street was closed and a "For Rent" sign was put on the property. Bob drove by the plant, noting the broken windows and the deterioration of the buildings. When he complained to the bank officer, he was politely told that he was only a beneficiary. Under the terms of the trust, the bank was in full charge of the business; and the goal of the trustee was to minimize any loss, not to run a competitive textile mill.

It also was clear that neither Bob nor his brother would have children to participate in the final distribution of trust assets. Elizabeth was nearly twenty years older than Bob. She had been his kindergarten teacher. They married when Bob was only fifteen years old. People said the marriage would not last. Bob's brother was homosexual. Ernie lived in center city with Victor, a younger man whom he met in Puerto Rico. At one point, Ernie formally adopted Victor as his son. Shortly afterward, Ernie received a letter from the trustee-bank telling him that an adopted son did not qualify to share in the distribution of the Boger Trust. The only final beneficiaries under Fredericka's trust would be the children of her daughter – but then, only if they outlived Bob, Ernie, and their mother. On the rare occasions when the Boger family got together, Bob had the sense that his nieces and nephews were mentally calculating when he, Ernie, and their mother would pass on from this vale of tears so that the nieces and nephews could collect the value of the trust fund. And, of course, in the event of Bob's death, Elizabeth would not qualify for any payment at all from the trust. Elizabeth would be on her own.

In the meanwhile, Bob and Ernie both approached the trustee each year, seeking additional payouts from the principal of the trust for the purpose of paying their income taxes. There was no dire need for the additional money. Bob had substantial balances in his savings and investment accounts. However, it was important to Bob that he increase the value of his personal investments so that Elizabeth would have something to fall back on in the event of Bob's death. Even though the requests for principal invasion were usually allowed, it was a demeaning process. In effect, the trust pitted the interests of the income beneficiaries against the interests of the final beneficiaries. Bob felt like Oliver Twist asking for more from an impersonal administrator who doled out the diminishing trust assets in an autocratic manner. Bob could not understand why the assets of the trust could not be divided among all the beneficiaries in equitable amounts and distributed immediately.

When it came time to draft Bob Boger's will, I wrote it exactly as he directed. Almost immediately, I received a message from George Nofer, the partner who then headed my firm's wills and estates department. The message said, "Gerry, please explore with your client the substantial tax benefits that would accrue to him through the creation of a testamentary trust." Bob laughed and, in his high-pitched voice said, "You can tell your Mr. Nofer that I am sure I can find a lawyer who will write this will the way I want it – without any trusts." Elizabeth smiled, and nodded her agreement.

You do not have to be an estates lawyer to know that, at some time, each of us will die. And you do not have to be a lawyer to know that human beings are particularly poor judges as to which of us will go first. Bob had retired early in response to medical advice about a serious illness. He and Elizabeth spent a substantial part of their remaining years transferring ownership of their assets from one name to the other as Bob's health worsened, and as Elizabeth's age advanced close to and beyond statistical life expectancy. In the meanwhile, Ernie was the first to go.

One afternoon, I received a call from Bob telling me that he had not heard from Ernie for more than a week. He went to Ernie's house but no one answered the door. He checked the police and hospitals to no avail. Did I know of any way to locate a missing person? A few days later, Bob called to tell me that he had just talked to Victor Boger. Victor said that Ernie died of a heart attack, and that according to Ernie's wishes his remains were cremated without notice to anyone. It was only after the cremation and burial were completed that Victor was permitted to tell anyone what happened. Bob was disappointed, but he said that it sounded like Ernie, and if that is what he wanted, that is the way it would be. Ernie's share of the trust income now shifted to Bob and his sister.

I knew that Elizabeth's health was deteriorating when she was hospitalized on successive occasions. Bob said that she was losing her cognitive capability. "She has even forgotten how to make soup. And all that takes is to open the can and add water." The effect of her dementia on their marriage was devastating. Bob said that it was like living with a different person. Eventually, the dementia prevailed and Elizabeth passed away at the age of 92-years. Contrary to the predictions at the time of their wedding, the marriage held up pretty well.

It was not too long after Elizabeth's death that Bob called to let me know that he planned to remarry. He wanted me to draft an antenuptual agreement. That is a contract that sets forth the property rights of the parties to an impending marriage. It also meant that I had to learn the law of such agreements. It was one more learning process that I trace to my dealings with Bob Boger. I don't know why an antenuptual agreement was such a big deal; he planned to leave Fay his entire estate. He said, "The money came from North Carolina, and it might just as well go back there when I'm gone."

Fay Magee was an old friend. Bob met her many years earlier when he spent several months of each year working in Boger & Crawford's North Carolina plant. The area was called "Boger City." Fay worked in the mill. At that time her name was Fay Oxford. An old photograph showed a pert, dark-haired girl with sparkling eyes. The present-day Fay was obviously in her seventies. She looked tired, but the eyes still sparkled. Fay Magee's husband died recently after a long marriage. In the wake of the death of their spouses, Bob and Fay renewed their friendship by correspondence, and then by visiting each other's homes. Before long, they decided to marry. They planned to alternate their time between Bob's home in Lower Gwynedd and Fay's home in Valdes (pronounced "Valdese").

    Within a few years, Bob's money went back to North Carolina as he had planned. He just did not expect it to happen so soon. Fay stayed in Lower Gwynedd for a few more years, and then went back to North Carolina. For Fay, it was a difficult experience. She lost two husbands in a stretch of about three years. The last I heard, Bob's nieces and nephews – now approaching their sixties – were still waiting for their chance to share in the Boger Trust.

    I was surprised at Bob's burial. I thought that he would be buried with Elizabeth. She was buried in the Haddon family plot as she had requested. Bob, the old Deutscher, is buried in the Boger family plot in the same cemetery in Frankford, about two miles north of the textile mill. Lieber Deutschland!

A TOAST TO TOM WILSON

Thomas Dudley Wilson was a member of the 25th Officer Candidates Course at Marine Corps Base, Quantico, Virginia, in the fall of 1959. I did not know him at that time. We were assigned to different units. In December 1959, we were both commissioned as second lieutenants in the same ceremony. It was a large function; more than 300 officers were commissioned that afternoon. I have no recollection of seeing Tom Wilson at the commissioning. On the other hand, I do remember him from The Basic School, although we were not in the same classes. In all probability he was one of the few married officers. Most of them lived off the base in one of the nearby towns. In any event, after more than nine months in the Marine Corps, Tom Wilson and I had much in common but we did not know each other.

Wilson looked like a Marine. He was tall, slender, and athletic in appearance. I suppose that I was no different from any other junior officer at The Basic School when I compiled a mental pecking order of my classmates, identifying those whom I would want to have under my command and those whom I would rather see assigned to someone else. Tom Wilson ranked pretty high on my list. Parenthetically, I have often wondered how we were rated by the Basic School staff officers. Such rating must have been a part of their job, but that information was not shared with us. Similarly, it is not clear how our future assignments were determined.

At the conclusion of The Basic School, we were instructed to submit three choices for our first assignment. As best I can recall at this late date, there were four options: (a) East Coast; (b) West Coast; (c) Okinawa; and (d) Sea Duty. Sea Duty was a "dress blues" assignment that included guard duty aboard ship and at embassies throughout the globe. Rumor had it that the first choice was rarely granted – unless the first choice happened to be Okinawa. I made Sea Duty my first choice, hoping against hope that I would not get it. Sea Duty was too much spit and polish for my blood. Nonetheless, I was hoping that a denial of my first choice would enhance the likelihood of my getting either the second or third picks, West Coast or East Coast. I was delighted when my orders came through assigning me to Camp Pendleton on the west coast. I should have known better.

Camp Pendleton is a magnificent location on the southern coast of California, roughly mid-way between Los Angeles and San Diego. That location also makes it a major transition point for Marine units going from the United States to the Third Marine Division on the island of Okinawa. "Konichi-wa Marine!" Pendleton was intended to be just a stepping stone on my jaunt to the Far East. An unfortunate automobile accident changed the plan. I showed up about a week late, after a short stay at Balboa Naval Hospital. By that time, another junior officer filled the slot intended for me in an infantry battalion slated for Okinawa. I took the next open spot which happened to be in an antitank battalion that was headed toward extinction. The following year, I was transferred to a desk job in Service Battalion, which was located in the mainside area of Pendleton. With slightly more than a year left on my active military commitment, it looked like Service Battalion would be my last duty assignment in the Marine Corps. That was when I got a phone call from Tom Wilson.

It must have been a tough call for Tom. He was not sure that I would remember him. There seemed to be a sense of urgency in his voice, reminiscent of Willy Loman in "Death of a Salesman." From his standpoint, this promised to be a tough sell. Tom said that he was assigned to an infantry battalion in Camp San Mateo, in the northern part of Pendleton. The battalion was scheduled to sail to Okinawa in

January, and it would commence its final phase of training in just two weeks. He said that the 13-month overseas tour of duty would play havoc with his marriage. He was trying to find another officer of the same grade who would be willing to switch assignments. Tom knew that the situation required more than just willingness.

My assignment at Service Battalion required a background in embarkation. Tom said that he would gladly attend the next class. Also, any officer who switched places with him would have to be on active duty until at least March 1963. My tour of duty would end in December 1962. Tom suggested that a three-month extension would almost certainly be approved. Of course, any switch would have to be approved by the commanders of both battalions. Finally, there was a practical aspect.

I not only had a soft desk job, but I also had a very comfortable apartment on top of the bluffs at the northern end of San Clemente, which gave me a great place to sit and watch the sun set over the Pacific Ocean during my final year on active duty. I was tempted to tell Tom that I was not interested in his proposal – but I did not say that. I said, "Give me a couple days to think about it. I will get back to you."

As things turned out, I did not watch the passage of 1962 from my picturesque vantage atop the cliffs of San Clemente. Instead, I crossed the International Date Line, wandered through the streets of Tokyo, Hong Kong and Manila, climbed the slopes of Mt. Fuji, and visited dozens of small villages in Japan, the Philippines and Okinawa. Between visits to those exotic places, I enjoyed first class accommodations on the following ships:

USS General William Mitchell (AP-114)
USS Bayfield (APA-33)

USS Talladega (APA-208)
USS Paul Revere (APA-248)
USS Montrose (APA-212)
USS Pickaway (APA-222)
USS Tulare (AKA-112)
USS George Clymer (APA-27)
USS Catamount (LSD-35)
USS Alamo (LSD-33)
USS Valley Forge (LPH-8)

Those are the kinds of places and things that people expect of Marines. In my mind, it was made possible by that unexpected phone call back in 1961.

So here's to you Tom Wilson – and the missus and the kids. I hope that service battalion was all that you expected, and that you enjoyed your remaining time in the Corps. As for me, I have no doubt; I got the best of the deal.

THE AMBASSADOR FOR SOCCER

In the 1940s, the Kensington neighborhood of Philadelphia was a hotbed of soccer. Jack Dunn was one of those Kensington kids who grew up with a soccer ball at his feet on Lighthouse Field. Moreover, Dunn was pretty good at the game. At Temple University, he was a 4-year All American. He played on the U.S. Olympic soccer team in 1952; and narrowly missed selection to the 1956 Olympic team. After his discharge from the army in 1958, Dunn took a sales job with Gulf Oil Company in Philadelphia. At about the same time, he was offered a part-time position as head coach of the St. Joseph's College soccer team. It was an offer that any sane person could refuse.

St. Joseph's had no soccer history. The new coach would have to organize the soccer program, recruit the team, coach the players, and lead St. Joe's soccer into the future. If Dunn wanted to stay in touch with the soccer world, there were many more attractive opportunities with

Jim Gavaghan, Jay Crawford, Sergio Tobia, Alex Pali, Jack Dunn, Jack Walls.

established soccer programs. But Dunn surprised everyone. He accepted the St. Joseph's job; held it for 26 years; and is now a member of the Saint Joseph's University Athletics Hall of Fame.

A few years ago, at a dinner honoring fifty years of Saint Joseph's soccer, Jim Gavaghan, Jay Crawford and Sergio Tobia asked Coach Dunn why he took the head coaching job back in 1958. There was no hesitation. Extending his index finger toward the questioners, Jack rattled off the points that everyone assumed would make the position unattractive: the college had no soccer experience; players would need to be recruited; players would need to be coached; schedules needed to be created; a tradition needed to be shaped. "I would be an ambassador for soccer," he said. "My father always told us that we should be ambassadors for soccer – promoting the game and generating interest in it. This was my chance to start a new college soccer tradition. It was just the kind of thing my father was talking about."

Interestingly, things were not always that harmonious between Jack Dunn and his father. When Jack graduated from Northeast Public High School – the one at 7th Street & Lehigh Avenue – the elder Dunn wanted Jack to go to Penn State and play for the legendary Walt Bahr, who had been captain of the national team that defeated England in a World Cup match. Jack did go to Penn State – for one week. He did not like it at State College. He packed up his things; returned home and called Temple's soccer coach, asking if there was still room on the team. Jack's father was livid. In his mind, Jack had insulted a local hero. Mr. Dunn refused to speak to his son. "He started to talk to me again when I made the Olympic team," said Jack. One suspects that Mr. Dunn would also have liked the title of Ambassador for St. Joe's Soccer.

THE SMALL CASE LAWYER

In the late 1960s, the conventional wisdom was that a young lawyer could get practical trial experience by handling cases with relatively small amounts in controversy – cases like those that the Philadelphia courts automatically assigned to compulsory arbitration before panels of three lawyers. In those days, that meant cases with a verdict potential of $3,000 or less. The arbitrators were paid about $100 each to decide a block of three cases. The chairman of the panel received a slightly larger amount because the chairman had the responsibility to arrange for a hearing room, to schedule the hearings, and to file the awards. As a general matter, the arbitration panels were comprised of three main interest groups: (1) lawyers specializing in plaintiffs' personal injury cases; (2) lawyers specializing in insurance defense cases; and (3) senior lawyers who were retired or close to retirement and who were satisfied with a short stress-free task and the relatively small compensation. In the late 1960s and early 1970s, I fell into the category of a novice trying to gain trial experience by handling small cases, particularly on the defense side of the issue.

Major Philadelphia law firms did not particularly favor the handling of small cases. Management wanted young lawyers to spend virtually all of their time working on menial tasks in large litigation cases, where major clients would pay major dollars for every minute of that time. Small cases generated little revenue. On the other hand, the small case client viewed his case as being just as important as the matters the firm was handling for United Parcel Service and AT&T. Between these two extremes was a senior lawyer who attracted the small case representation and often assigned it to me. In effect, George P. Williams, III said, "I'll back you up with management but don't let me down." George brought in many such small cases.

Granite Mutual Insurance Company was one of the small insurance companies that regularly assigned the defense of its claims to George Williams. The corporate counsel for Granite Mutual was Warner Earnshaw, who – much to his chagrin – was commonly known as "the brother of George Earnshaw," a World Series pitcher for Connie Mack's Philadelphia Athletics back in the 1930s. Warner did not expect George Williams personally to handle all of Granite Mutual's cases, but he did expect those cases to be handled competently, regardless of who conducted the trial. That expectation persisted even when the case involved a rear-end automobile accident and our client was the hittor and not the hittee.

In this case, the evidence clearly showed that the damage to our insured's vehicle was in the front and the damage to the plaintiff's car was at the rear bumper, smack in the middle. Fortunately for Granite Mutual, a police accident investigation report stated that a Philadelphia street sweeper saw the accident and said that the plaintiff's car turned right onto Fitzwater Street, suddenly stopped, and abruptly backed into my client's vehicle, which had come to a stop at the intersection. The police report also said that the two occupants of the car – the plaintiffs in this case – were a mother and daughter who were spending the day making arrangements for the daughter's wedding. Thus, the facts supported the theory that the two women were so preoccupied with their shopping spree that they failed to notice they had turned the wrong way into a one-way street. The street sweeper's testimony was eminently credible, but whose version of the story would the arbitrators believe?

I advised the chairman of the arbitration panel that he could hold the hearing in one of my firm's conference rooms at 2:00 p.m. in the afternoon. Immediately after the arbitration was scheduled, I received a notice for a deposition in one of my major cases. The deposition was scheduled for 10:00 a.m. on the same day as the arbitration hearing. The deposition was expected to be short. I thought that I could handle both events without asking for a postponement. I subpoenaed the street sweeper to come to my office at 1:00 p.m., leaving me an hour to prepare him to testify.

It was close. The deposition went longer than expected but I was back in the Packard Building by about 1:15 p.m. The receptionist smiled when she told me that a gentleman was waiting for me in my office. Gary Wynkoop was standing near the receptionist, but he was not smiling – Gary was laughing. Gary seemed to thrive on the competition for advancement among the associates within the law firm. He particularly seemed to enjoy it when I was faced with a difficult situation. "I thought it would be best if your witness waited for you in your office, rather than the lobby area," he said as he followed me down the hall.

When I opened the office door, I was surprised that the lights were out. Then I heard the faint snoring. My witness was sound asleep. He was a short, slender man in his mid forties. He was wearing work clothes that were covered with a layer of dust. He was also very intoxicated. In those days, the popular comic strip "Peanuts" featured an unkempt character named "Pigpen," who gave off a small puff of dust every time he moved an arm or a leg. This mild-mannered little man with the whiskey smile reminded me very much of Pigpen. In another thirty minutes, Pigpen would be the key witness for my defense case. No wonder Gary Wynkoop was laughing.

As the lawyers and witnesses were entering the arbitration hearing room, I called aside the chairman of the arbitration panel and the lawyer who represented the plaintiffs. I told them that I had subpoenaed an independent witness over whom I had no control, and I was worried about how he might conduct himself if he had to sit through a long drawn-out hearing before it was his turn to testify. I suggested that we modify the usual procedure and allow the street sweeper to be the first witness, after which he would be free to leave and we could continue the hearing in the normal course. The chairman and the plaintiffs' lawyer glanced across the room at Pigpen, and quickly agreed to the suggestion.

All three members of the arbitration panel were senior in age. They were hoping for a quick hearing so they could catch an early train home. The mother and daughter plaintiffs were accompanied by the father. All of them were dressed in their Sunday finest. The driver of my client's vehicle also wore a coat and tie. The chairman motioned to Pigpen to come to the head of the table and sit next to the panel. After administering an oath and identifying the witness, the chairman signaled to me to proceed.

I began in a routine manner,
"Mr. witness, do you recall an automobile accident that occurred at 16th and Fitzwater Streets, on May 7th, three years ago?"
The response was, "Sheee—it, do I!"

I tried not to smile. Over the next five minutes, Pigpen described the accident in very colorful language. When he finished his description, no one dared to ask him any more questions. "If there are no more questions," intoned the chairman, "the witness is excused." Turning to Pigpen, the chairman added, "Mr. witness, you may leave now." "Do I have to?" Pigpen asked. The chairman hesitated and then said, "No, this is a public proceeding. You can stay if you want to." And so he stayed.

When the mother moved to the head of the table to testify, Pigpen sat in the chair that she vacated – right next to the father. When the mother testified about the accident, Pigpen laughed and slapped the father on the back, saying, "Y'hear her? Y'hear what she said?" So it went for the next hour. It was a show within a show. To make matters even better, the panel's award was in favor of my client.

It is hard to say what it is that prompts a jury or an arbitration panel to rule in favor of one party and against another. I am convinced that one critical aspect of the situation is effective communication. In the case just described, Pigpen was certainly not a communications expert, but his sincerity and humor were pervasive. Moreover, he had no monetary interest in the outcome of the case. He was like Jiminy Cricket. He was the common sense conscience that appealed to the arbitrators. The arbitrators believed him.

A similar situation arose in a case for Rockwood Insurance Company. Rockwood insured a construction business in North Philadelphia. The complaint alleged that the company's workmen arrived at 3125 N. Carlisle Street at approximately 8:00 a.m. It was a destitute part of the city. Most of the homes were in a severe state of disrepair. On this day, the workmen entered the premises at 3125 and quickly gutted the interior rooms so that the workmen who would follow could install new walls, floors and ceilings. According to the complaint, after about three hours one of the workmen shouted to the others that they were in the wrong house. They were supposed to gut the premises at 3325 N. Carlisle, two blocks up the street. The men then climbed into their truck and drove away. In the meanwhile, the property at 3125 was destroyed and its owner wanted to be paid for the damages.

The construction company turned out to be a one-man business. That one-man was Fred, a slender 23-year old

African-American who was born and raised in the North Philadelphia neighborhood where the incident occurred. Fred was an independent contractor who dealt with local real estate developers who were rehabilitating deteriorated buildings. Fred's crew would do the rough demolition work and clear the debris from the premises so that the higher paid skilled construction workers – the carpenters, plumbers and electricians – could complete their work without any wasted time. Depending on the size of the job, Fred would hire friends to work on a per diem basis. One of those friends accompanied Fred to the arbitration hearing. Both wore khaki work trousers and T-shirts.

The arbitrators were all experienced lawyers. There were two men and one woman. Two of them regularly represented plaintiffs, and the other specialized in insurance defense. The plaintiff's evidence was pretty bland. The occupant of the house next door said that workmen went into 3125 N. Carlisle and began pulling the place apart. Then, shortly before noon they drove away. The owner of the building said that, after learning of the incident, he drove around the neighborhood and located a crew about a block away. He identified the crew through Fred's pickup truck.

Fred was the only witness for the defense. You can take the man out of North Philadelphia but you cannot take North Philadelphia out of the man. The English teachers at Edison High School would have cringed had they heard Fred speak. It was classic neighborhood-talk. Forget about grammar. Forget about pronunciation and enunciation. Forget about all that jazz. Fred talked like he always talked. And the amazing thing was that he was crystal clear. All of us understood exactly the thoughts that he conveyed. He had a gift for effective oral communication.

Fred said that he did not do any work at either 3125 or 3325 N. Carlisle. The day of the alleged incident was a

Saturday and Fred didn't work on Saturdays. On Saturday, his pickup truck was parked outside his house all day. He emphasized the accuracy of his testimony by reminding the panel that his was a one-man business. "I am the contractor!" he said. On cross-examination, plaintiff's lawyer searched frantically for a way to impeach Fred's testimony. "Isn't it possible," he asked, "that your friend used your pickup truck that day?" For about three seconds, Fred stared at the lawyer as though he could not believe that someone had asked such an absurd question. And then, waving his right arm in the direction of his friend, Fred said, "He ain't no contractor! I'm the contractor! I got the pickup truck! If he wants to be a contractor, he can get his own pickup truck." The arbitrators were smiling. They entered their award in favor of Fred.

Some mornings I am tempted to go out and buy a pickup truck. Then I could be a contractor too.

II.PHILADELPHIA LAWYERS

These five articles try to capture the personalities of lawyers who made a difference to me. Three articles were published by the Philadelphia Lawyer Magazine. Another was accepted for publication but withdrawn due to an objection by a member of the family.

It is one thing to read a quantitative list of lawyerly accomplishments; it is quite another to appreciate each lawyer's personality. There should be more articles of this type. Old friends should not be forgotten.

PRINCE ALBERT

Prince Albert was a popular brand of pipe tobacco. It was sold in eye-catching red cans with the picture of an elegant gentleman, presumably Prince Albert, on the label. A very, very old joke was to ask a shopkeeper whether he had Prince Albert in a can. An affirmative response would trigger the punch line, "Well for god's sake, let him out!" One unintended result of this overused joke was that a lot of people named Albert became known as "Prince" Albert. Al Sheppard seemed to like the nickname.

It has been nearly sixty years since Tony Salvitti introduced me to his North Catholic classmate Al Sheppard. There was nothing about Sheppard's appearance or manner that would set him apart as exceptional; but Tony said that Al finished first in his high school class, and had a scholarship to Villanova to study engineering. He also played the piano and wrote music. Not long afterward, I was one of a group of politically connected college students that conducted a traffic survey for the Pennsylvania Department of Transportation. Al Sheppard was also a part of that group, but our interests ran in different directions. Along with Jim Gavaghan and Jay Kuvik, I looked for basketball games at nearby recreation centers. Al was more interested in getting to South Philadelphia to see a girl that he knew. The traffic survey ended in September. It was more than eight years before I saw Sheppard again.

After mustering out of the Marine Corps in 1963, I took a job with the Redevelopment Authority of Philadelphia. My office was in the Lumbermens Building, across Broad

Street from the Bellevue Stratford Hotel. Al Sheppard also worked in the Lumbermens Building. He had finished a four-year tour in the U.S. Navy, and was working as an engineer for the Philadelphia Electric Company. Two years later, when I enrolled for law school in the evening division of Temple University, I was surprised to find that Al Sheppard was in the class ahead of me.

Going to law school at night was like going through boot camp in the Marine Corps, except for the age and experience of the participants. It was a four-year program of classes, five nights per week, and preparation for classes (i.e., homework) took up about half of the weekends. At the end of each work day, we would hop on the Broad Street subway and take it to the Temple campus at Columbia Avenue. The law school was in a drab two-story building called Reber Hall. In the basement was a small room that the students used as a coffee and smoking area while waiting for the start of classes. Classes ended at about 8:30 p.m., after which we scurried back to the Broad Street subway and a long ride home. During these excursions, Al Sheppard and I had ample time to discuss our divergent experiences in the military, particularly during the Cuban Missile Crisis when Al was on the USS Furse, a destroyer off the coast of Cuba, and I was on the USS Valley Forge, a helicopter carrier off the coast of China.

Typically, the first year class in the evening law school numbered about 75 students. By the second year, the class size was reduced to about twenty. The annual attrition continued at a less severe rate up until the year of graduation. In the meanwhile, the survivors clung to each other and the four classes often merged with each other for social activities. One of the main activities was a charitable effort by the wives of the law students to provide Christmas gifts for needy children of the prisoners in Eastern State Prison. Another activity, more appreciated by the overworked students, was the Friday night get-togethers after class.

The word was spread among all four classes where we would meet after the last class. It might be at the Pike Pub at Broad and Pike Streets, or at Sylvie's at 11th & Wolf, or at the Officers Club at the Navy Yard where Al Sheppard, Tim Kittredge and I were members, or at a host of other places. Lord, did we look forward to those Friday nights.

In my first year of law school, the course on contracts was generally recognized as the course that resulted in the most failures, and Dr. Eldon Magaw had the reputation of being the "hatchet man." Dr. Magaw based his contracts course on the Restatement of Contracts, which sets out approximately 366 specific rules, each based on court decisions and general principles of law. Dr. Magaw thought he was doing us a favor when he gave the final exam – the only exam – in two parts. The first part, which would count for nearly 90% of our final grade, would be given shortly after Easter. I could not believe that the full year's grade would be based on just that one examination, but that was what Dr. Magaw said; and that is what he did. Three days before the exam, I put my contracts textbook and notes in the middle of my desk at work, and camouflaged them with Redevelopment Authority papers. Thus situated, I studied for that exam for three full days.

On the evening of the contracts exam, as I emerged from the Broad Street subway and walked up the steps to Reber Hall, the first person I met was Al Sheppard. He said that I looked worried, and asked what was the problem. When I told him about the contracts exam, he said that there was no reason to worry. All I had to do was remember the Restatements – and he went on to recite them word for word. Worse yet, he then cited the cases upon which the Restatements were based. And this was a course that he had taken a full year earlier. It was my introduction to how his classmates must have viewed their academic competition with Al Sheppard. Al was far and away first in his law school class.

In Al's last year of law school, we had some of the same classes and, for those classes Al joined with my study group that included Gary Wynkoop, Ray Cullen and Joe Coffey. By that time, Gary, Ray and I were working full-time as paralegals in the prestigious firm of Morgan, Lewis & Bockius. Still, we could not keep up with Al's intellect and memory – it was frustrating. On the other hand, Joe Coffey would often plead with us to stop our griping about Sheppard because, "I am here to learn enough law from the four of you so that I can pass the exam." Invariably, someone would respond that when all was said and done, Joe would probably make more money than the four of us combined. Darned if that isn't exactly what happened.

After graduation from law school, Al Sheppard, Gary Wynkoop and I accepted offers from the same law firm, Schnader, Harrison, Segal & Lewis. Al worked mainly on the Pfizer tetracycline antitrust case. The hours were long, and the issues were complex, but Al seemed to thrive on those challenges. Most of my work was for other clients. As a result, we did not see much of each other at the office. However, in our spare time, both Al and I volunteered to help out the Democratic Party in Lansdowne. The Democrats in Lansdowne needed help. Voter registration was at least two-to-one in favor of the Republicans. Al came up with the idea of filing a taxpayer suit against the Republican-dominated Borough of Lansdowne.

At a poorly attended borough council meeting, the council adopted a tax increase but made no public announcement of what it had done because the councilmen feared that it would sway voters against them in the coming election. The day after that election, the increased tax bills arrived in the mail. The borough residents were furious. Several of them volunteered to have a lawsuit brought in their names. Al chose as the lead plaintiff a Lansdowner named John L. Sullivan. It was the name of the last bare knuckles heavyweight boxing champion. The case is recorded in the court docket as *John L. Sullivan v. The Borough of Lansdowne*. We told everyone that it was the court's last bare knuckles fight. As a practical matter, we did not stand a chance. Nonetheless, it was our first time in court and we held our own against experienced opposition.

If we did not know it before then, we now knew that the practice of law is a pressure-driven endeavor that can adversely affect anyone who gets close to it. Statistics show that lawyers are especially susceptible to addiction to both drugs and alcohol. Gradually, it became more and more apparent that Al Sheppard was becoming one of those statistics. On occasion, Al would call and say that he was not in the office but could I pick up his paycheck and drop it off at his home (which was just three blocks from my house). Those occurrences became more and more frequent. Finally, the firm's administrative partner called me in and instructed me to stop doing things for Al. He said that the firm consulted experts on alcoholism and their advice was to force the addict to stand on his own two feet.

One evening at about 6:30 p.m., I was getting ready to go home when I noticed Al sitting at his desk, staring off into space. I asked if something was wrong. Al said that he would not be able to get home. He said that there were a couple of taprooms on the route and that he could not help but stop in and have a drink. Once he did that, he would be there all night or maybe out all night with friends he met there. It was hard to believe that the strongest willed person I knew could not overcome such a simple temptation.

Rosemary Cullen understood that compulsion. Rosemary was George Williams' secretary; she was in her late forties. She had once been a pianist at a cocktail bar. Everyone in the law firm knew of Rosemary's involvement with Alcoholics Anonymous. I once saw Rosemary interrupt George in the middle of dictation, and then tell him that she would be back in an hour to finish his letter – after her A.A. meeting. George roared out that this was a law office and that the letter he was dictating was important. As Rosemary rushed out the door, she screamed back over her shoulder, "My A.A. meeting is important too!" Rosemary explained Al Sheppard's situation to us.

Alcoholics Anonymous has a 12-step program which is based on the proposition that addiction is an illness which the victim is powerless to overcome, except with the help of God. The program is effectuated by regular meetings of support groups that encourage A.A. members to follow the twelve steps each day, one day at a time. Rosemary said that Al would have to hit rock bottom and then, if he bought into the A.A. program, he might be able to work his way back. There were no guarantees of recovery. On the other hand, it was virtually guaranteed that the present course of conduct would lead to the loss of Al's job with the Schnader law firm. He lost the job. He lost his marriage. And, to a great extent, he lost his self-respect. Al was the picture of abject despair.

It took a few years but Al began the long climb back with the help of a few friends who did not forget him. Marv Factor, a law school classmate, and Tom Monteverde, a former Schnader partner, employed Al in their law firms. Although Tom Monteverde is not a demanding person, he is an outstanding lawyer who sets a high standard for the lawyers associated with him. Day after day, month after month, and year after year, Sheppard met those high standards of lawyering.

Bernie and Bob Avellino, Al's brothers-in-law, provided the political savvy that got Al on the ballot as a candidate for judge of the Court of Common Pleas. But it was up to Al to deal with the news reporters and questions about alcoholism. Al met the issue head-on. He rejected their suggestion that he was a "recovered alcoholic." He said that there is no such thing. He said that he continues to fight alcoholism every day; and he continues to recognize that the battle is never over. That was nearly thirty years ago.

Al is not the only lawyer who successfully overcame addiction – John Rogers Carroll also comes to mind. John founded a very successful bar association program to help lawyers deal with addiction. But unlike Sheppard and Carroll, most lawyers in recovery cling to that second A, anonymity. It is an understandable instinct, but it also means that there are precious few role models who can demonstrate to lawyers struggling with addiction that the illness strikes even the most talented members of the profession, that it can be overcome and that the victim can be restored to a high level of legal accomplishment.

The judicial accomplishments of Albert W. Sheppard, Jr. in the Court of Common Pleas of Philadelphia are now a matter of record. He was elected to three consecutive 10-year terms. During his term in family court that dealt with child abuse and delinquency, he was known for maintaining a container of lollypops for the children who had the misfortune to come before that court. When he was transferred to the civil trial division, he was a leading part of a committee that recommended improvements to the operation of the civil courts. He was embarrassed when the media referred to those recommendations as being originated by "The Sheppard Committee." He was also a leader in the innovation of a "Commerce Court." He received many awards, including the Justice William J. Brennan, Jr. Distinguished Jurist Award from the Philadelphia Bar Association, and the Golden Crowbar Award from the Pennsylvania Conference of State Trial Judges.

I did not see too much of Al Sheppard during his years on the bench. Another of the A.A. rules requires members to avoid those persons who were part of his past drinking environment. Our Friday night law school soirees qualified me to be treated as a near occasion of sin. A good judge plays by the rules; and Al was a good judge. Despite that no-contact rule, on many a November 10th before my retirement, my phone would ring. I would pick it up and hear: "Mr. St. John, this is Judge Sheppard's secretary. Judge Sheppard wants to talk to you. Hold on, please." [ring] "Gerry, I am speaking low because I am in court. I just wanted to wish you a Happy Marine Corps Birthday! You jarheads are all alike."

I'll miss Prince Albert.

GEORGE THE THIRD

The old central YMCA at 1421-25 Arch Street was a convenient location for those of us who used our lunch break for exercise. On a balcony above one end of the basketball court was a small, steeply banked running track. The sign on the wall said that 26 laps around the track was the equivalent of one mile. I was finishing my workout when I noticed a tall man in his mid-forties come out of the weight room and onto the track. He looked tired. His gray-streaked black hair was beginning to fall down over his forehead. He lumbered forward in a heavy-footed manner. One of the regulars at the Y caught my attention, pointed to the newcomer and whispered, "Do you know who that is? That's George P. Williams, III! He's one of the city's best trial lawyers."

At the time, the name meant nothing to me. I had just started evening law school and I was not yet familiar with Philadelphia's lawyers. Vaguely, I remembered the 1955 mayoral election when a young Thacher Longstreth, challenged the Republican Party leadership and upset its endorsed candidate in the primary election. I also recalled that Thacher was then soundly defeated by Richardson Dilworth in the main election. But I had forgotten that the Republican Party's endorsed candidate that year was George P. Williams, III.

George P. Williams, III

Four years after that encounter at the YMCA, I joined the Schnader law firm where George Williams was a senior partner and a member of the executive committee. Everyone called him "George the Third," to distinguish him from his father, George P. Williams, Jr., who was counsel to the firm. George the Third had a presence that dominated a room. In his blue pinstripe suit, he looked taller than six feet, four inches, and his broad shoulders and large, beefy hands suggested a weight much heavier than the 220-pound limit that he set for himself. Those imposing physical dimensions were complemented by a booming baritone voice that worked in perfect syncopation with the gestures of his large hands. But his most noticeable features were a wide smile and an irrepressible sense of humor. Like comedian Red Skelton, George laughed at his own jokes – and he laughed harder than anyone else.

George was quick to quote the Bible, for example, characterizing an opponent's argument as being similar to the "Law of the Medes and the Persians," that once adopted could not be changed even by the King. And he was always on the alert for a multi-syllable word that he could spring on an unsuspecting court or an opponent during the course of a trial. When an adversary complained emotionally to the court about an aspect of George's trial tactics, George simply shrugged his shoulders, leaned back in his chair and said, "Your honor, I am not the least bit offended by the *hortatory excoriations* of opposing counsel." And then he doubled up in laughter at his own obtuse language. Pretty soon opposing counsel was laughing too.

George rarely criticized an opponent. "I can't do that," he said, "I taught most of them. They are only doing what I taught them." There was something to that. George P. Williams, III taught torts at Temple Law School for nearly 15 years. His connection with Temple came about because of the Second World War. Up until that time, the Williams family had a long-standing relationship with the University of Pennsylvania. Consistent with the expectations of his family, George graduated from the Wharton School and proceeded on to "The Law School." (For the uninitiated, that means the University of Pennsylvania's Law School.) At the end of his first year, the country was at war. Like many other young men, George decided to enlist in the military. To his chagrin, none of the services would take him. The problem was an enlarged heart, a condition that the doctors attributed to his days as a high school wrestler. George was devastated. From all outward appearances, he was the picture of health. But this giant of a man was one of the few persons his age who was not in the military service. George decided that he would do his part for the country by taking a full-time job with the War Production Board. He withdrew from Penn but continued his legal education in the evening at Temple Law School. The change was an academic culture shock.

In 1942, Temple Law School was located on the 13th floor of the Gimbel Building at 9th and Chestnut Streets. George would later tell colleagues that one of the highlights of his law school experience was meeting Uncle WIP, a children's radio show personality, on the elevator. George graduated from Temple in 1944 and soon became an outstanding trial lawyer in his father's firm, Orr, Williams & Baxter. Meanwhile, as the war came to an end and servicemen returned from the war effort, Temple Law School was flooded with applications. George was offered a position teaching torts. From 1945 to 1960, he taught law at Temple while maintaining a full-time private practice of law.

George's dominating presence, his courtroom success and his gregarious sense of humor made him a favorite of the law students. Lawyers who attended his classes still talk of classroom exchanges such as the one where a hesitant young student asked, "Mr. Williams, is it okay if I smoke in the classroom during the break?" "Smoke?" responded George, "I don't care if you burst into flames!" That said, George Williams burst into laughter, as did the entire class.

In 1960, when Orr, Williams & Baxter merged with Schnader, George's stint as a teacher came to an end. At Schnader, George handled a wide variety of major trials: personal injury, antitrust, securities, public service regulation and, on at least one occasion he represented a major Philadelphia law firm. He was a "lawyers' lawyer," whose cheerful demeanor masked the meticulous preparation that went into every case. Every question, every word – written and oral – was thought out well in advance.

I was fortunate to be able to work with George Williams for nearly 14 years on a number of cases, including a series of rate cases for Bell of Pennsylvania and operating rights cases for United Parcel Service in the States of Arizona, New Mexico, Oklahoma and Utah. It quickly became apparent that George would not let his personal predilections interfere with the interests of his client. For example, in Santa Fe, New Mexico, the lawyer who represented the client's main opponent always wore a snow-white ten-gallon cowboy hat to the hearings. The hat was immaculate. He said that he bought a new hat every week so that he would not appear in the hearing room with a soiled hat. Throughout that entire hearing, George Williams suppressed a very strong urge to buy a black hat and wear it to the hearing. The case was too important to the client to risk the possibility that the hearing judge would be offended by the black hat or by George poking fun at one of Santa Fe's premier lawyers. Only after the hearings were concluded and we were at the airport on our way home, did George pose for photos wearing a wide grin and a large black "Chief Wahoo" hat, a Navajo chapeau with a very high crown, a flat circular brim and a beaded hat band that was immediately recognizable to anyone who read the popular comic strip L'il Abner. George looked like he was seven feet tall.

On the other hand, when George's personal instincts coincided exactly with the interests of the client, there was no question as to his approach. In a case where George was preparing a closing argument that addressed the credibility of the opposing party's main witness, an associate described how another lawyer had recently handled a similar argument in an indirect manner. "That's not me!" said George. "That kind of approach may work for some pixie-ish lawyers but I'm not Peter Pan." Smiling as he developed that thought, he added, " I can't go flitting around the courtroom like a fairy. People expect me to meet issues head-on. I've done pretty well by calling a spade a spade, and by swinging a big club. And that is what I am going to do here." He did that – and he won the verdict.

In 1983, George and I were defending Michelin Tire Corporation in a case that involved a motorcycle accident. Although the defense preparation was going well, the client had a notion that its defense might be improved if its lawyers were experienced motorcyclists. George Williams was not particularly enthusiastic about getting on a motorcycle. However, the client persisted and even rented a racecourse on Long Island for two days in June so that George and I could learn to operate a motorcycle. I was asked to notify George and to get his measurements for the leather jackets, trousers and gloves, and for the helmets that we would need in our training session. I sent George a memo requesting that information and, as an afterthought, added that he could have his preference for the back of the leather jacket: an eagle, a Jolly Roger, or a heart with the word "mother" inscribed across it. George responded by writing his extra-large measurements directly on the memo. At the bottom, he wrote:

"Among motorcyclists, 'mother' is only half a word. Please get me the full treatment."

George never made it to that motorcycle session.

May 16, 1983 was a fateful day. It was the best of days; it was the worst of days. It was the day that United Parcel Service held its annual meeting. One item on the agenda was the election of George P. Williams, III as a director of the company. In Philadelphia, George Williams and Brad Ward went to the Racquet Club for a short workout and lunch. While doing some mild calisthenics, George suddenly stiffened as if frozen in-place, and then collapsed to the floor. He was rushed to Graduate Hospital where he was pronounced dead. George the Third was only 62 years of age.

Shortly after George Williams' death, the Schnader Firm, together with many of George's partners, associates and friends, funded in Temple University School of Law an award that memorializes both his career as a trial lawyer and his distinguished teaching experience as a member of the Law School faculty. The George P. Williams, III, Memorial Award, is conferred annually on a full-time faculty member chosen by the graduating students for his or her outstanding excellence as a teacher. The income from the Memorial Fund is used to purchase books for the Temple University Library and each volume so purchased bears a George P. Williams, III, Memorial Fund bookplate which also identifies the faculty member honored in the year of the book's acquisition.

George got the full treatment.

A MORAL ISSUE

©Philadelphia Bar Association, reprinted with permission

The tide of civil rights ebbed and flowed for nearly three years after playing a critical role in the election of President John F. Kennedy. But in the spring of 1963, the mood became increasingly violent, and the focus of the nation was drawn south to Alabama. Racist elements resorted to explosives and death threats against African-American leaders. Law enforcement authorities not only refused to protect citizens who were conducting nonviolent marches in their quest for equal rights, but openly joined the opposition, using police dogs, night sticks and fire hoses to intimidate protesters.

Even the highest elected official in the state of Alabama, Governor George C. Wallace, announced that he would disregard the federal court order that prohibited interference with the admission of African-American students at the University of Alabama. Under the guise of testing the constitutionality of that order, Wallace vowed to stand in the doorway to prevent the integration of the university.

In many parts of the country, people viewed this sad series of events as a "Southern problem," one over which they had little influence and no control. However, some individuals saw it as their duty to speak out and to participate in the direction of government.

In Philadelphia, Geraldine Segal was not the least bit timid, "Well, what is the bar of the nation doing about this? What should *you* be doing?" Geraldine asked her lawyer husband, Bernard G. Segal, who, for perhaps the first time in his nearly 56 years, was speechless.

Segal took Gerry's challenge seriously, but he also knew the enormity of the problem. He took stock of the resources available to him. He was a former Chancellor of the Philadelphia Bar Association and an officer of the American Law Institute. He had been a key part of the effort that persuaded President Eisenhower to permit the ABA to pass on the qualifications of judicial candidates, and he had served as chairman of the ABA's Committee on the Federal Judiciary. During the Eisenhower years, he also struck up a friendship with Robert F. Kennedy, who was then working on the Senate investigation of the Teamsters. These activities had brought him into contact with many of the leaders of the legal community nationwide. But what could he do about the storm that was gathering in Alabama? It was Friday morning and Governor Wallace would be in the doorway of the Tuscaloosa campus the following Tuesday.

By the time he reached his office at 1719 Packard Building, Segal had a plan. He picked up his phone and called the two leading newspapers in Birmingham, Alabama. Would they reserve front-page space in Monday's edition for a statement endorsed by acknowledged leaders of the bar and addressed to Governor Wallace with respect to the situation at the University of Alabama? Both editors promised to reserve the space. Segal then recruited his partner, Jerome J. Shestack, and the two set about calling leaders of the bar across the country.

It was a long, arduous job. In the first instance, it took time to make personal contact. Friday soon faded into the weekend. Throughout the day Saturday, the calls continued. Over and over again the question was asked, "Would you join in a public statement to the effect that the governor of Alabama should comply with the lawful order of a federal court?" For many of those lawyers, the political and economic risks were enormous. Segal's heart and hopes occasionally plummeted as lawyers whom he had counted on to support the effort declined to participate. More often, however, spirits soared as increasing numbers of eminent lawyers joined the effort.

The last call was completed about 3 a.m. Sunday. A total of forty-six lawyers joined in the statement. Although they would issue the statement as individuals, they included the president of the American College of Trial Lawyers, three former attorneys general of the United States, the current president and six past presidents of the American Bar Association, the deans of the law schools of Harvard, Mississippi, North Carolina, Notre Dame, Penn and Yale, and a brother and law partner of one of Governor Wallace's closest advisers. The statement read in part as follows:

> "In a government of laws, the Governor is not free to flout the court's decree so long as it remains in force, particularly when the issues have been so recently and so frequently resolved by the highest court in the land.
>
> "Lawyers have a special responsibility to support the rule of law in our society and to obey the fundamental legal principles that guarantee safety and justice for all. To this end, as lawyers, we ask Governor Wallace to refrain from defiance of a solemn court order.

If he is present when the students present themselves for registration, we call on him to stand aside."

On Monday, June 10, 1963, the two Birmingham newspapers not only published the statement and the names of the forty-six prestigious lawyers, but also one of the papers, the *Birmingham News*, published a favorable editorial. The Associated Press carried the statement to newspapers nationwide.

On Tuesday, June 11, 1963, Governor Wallace took his position in the doorway at the University of Alabama. For a while, it was a game of cat and mouse in which neither side forced the issue. In the early afternoon, Deputy U.S. Attorney General Nicholas Katzenbach approached with two African-American students. After making a brief statement for the news media, Governor Wallace stepped aside and a confrontation was avoided. Katzenbach, along with Attorney General Robert Kennedy and President John F. Kennedy, later said that the forty-six-lawyer protest was a significant influence in weakening Governor Wallace's resistance.

That evening, President Kennedy went on television to report on the status of civil rights. Kennedy bluntly told the country: "We are confronted primarily with a moral issue. It is as old as the scriptures and is as clear as the American Constitution . . .. We face, therefore, a moral crisis as a country and as a people."

The President asked for the help of all citizens "to provide the kind of equality of treatment which we would want ourselves, to give a chance for every child to be educated to the limits of his talents."

Several days afterward, Robert Kennedy called Segal to thank the leaders of the bar for their active help in the crisis at the University of Alabama. During the conversation, Segal noted that President Kennedy had already reached out for support from leaders of other key groups, such as labor leaders, educators and businessmen, and he suggested that lawyers would also respond to such a call. Thirty minutes later, Segal received a call from Lee White, a member of the White House staff. White asked Segal to prepare a list of 250 lawyers, at least one from every state, Puerto Rico and the Virgin Islands, including the forty-six who had joined in the statement to Governor Wallace, and including at least fifty members of minority groups. They were to be invited to attend a White House conference for lawyers on the subject of civil rights.

Robert Kennedy later told Segal that President Kennedy would create a lawyers' committee for civil rights and that he wanted to appoint Segal as one of its co-chairmen. Segal was honored, but he declined the offer. It would be impossible. He had just completed an extensive period of service to the ABA, and the private practice of law created insuperable demands on his time.

On June 21, 1963, attendance at the conference in the East Room of the White House exceeded all expectations. Despite only four days' notice, 244 leaders of the bar from all areas of the country attended the session. Bernard Segal was among them. He stayed at the rear of the room, intending to return to Philadelphia at the close of the meeting. From his position, he felt almost detached from the important occasion that unfolded before him.

President Kennedy, Vice President Lyndon B. Johnson and Attorney General Robert F. Kennedy spoke to the assembled lawyers. President Kennedy emphasized the seriousness of the racial unrest pervading the nation in "this hour of moral and constitutional crisis." The President announced that he was creating a committee that would be known as the Lawyers' Committee for Civil Rights Under Law. The co-chairmen of the new committee would be "Harrison Tweed of New York City and Bernard G. Segal of Philadelphia."

Segal felt as though a bolt of lightning had coursed through him. He wanted to stand up and scream that he had said "No!" He could not possibly accept such an appointment.

When the meeting ended, Segal hurriedly made his way to the front of the room and sought out President Kennedy. He explained that there had been a mistake, that he had told Bobby that he could not accept the appointment, that he simply did not have enough time.

Kennedy responded that Bobby had reported those exact words. But Bobby also told the President about a visit to Segal's home, where he saw among Segal's memorabilia a note dating back to the third or fourth grade when Segal won an essay contest. The unsigned note had been on his desk when Bernie came back to the classroom after receiving the award. On it was written: "You Sheeny, you didn't win it – you stole it."

"Mr. Segal," said the President, "I want someone at the head of this committee who has experienced and lived with prejudice."
"But, Mr. President," Segal stammered, "that incident occurred a long time ago."
"Yes," the President replied, "but you kept that note all this time."
For the second time in his life, Bernard G. Segal was speechless.

Under the leadership of Segal and Tweed, the Lawyers' Committee for Civil Rights Under Law was a singular success. Its call for peaceful compliance with court orders had an immediate and persuasive impact. The committee also sent volunteer lawyers to Mississippi at the request of the National Council of Churches. Later, the committee opened an office in Jackson, Mississippi, and under very difficult circumstances, lawyers from all parts of the country, many of them from Philadelphia, participated in the higher calling of the bar.

John F. Kennedy was right. The civil rights crisis of 1963 was a moral issue, one that demanded a distinction between right and wrong. In his televised address to the American people in June 1963, Kennedy also said, "Those who do nothing are inviting shame as well as violence. Those who act boldly are recognizing right as well as reality."

The ability of each individual to make a difference in society, and the obligation of all persons to participate in a democratic government were recurring themes underlying the Kennedy administration. Those themes are also well known to Philadelphia lawyers.

FRANK B. MURDOCH:
A Reminiscence

©Philadelphia Bar Association, reprinted with permission.

    The Schnader law offices at 1719 Packard Building were pretty much what one might expect of a Philadelphia law firm in the 1960s. The dark walnut wood trim and doors, together with the green carpeting, the interior location and dim lighting, reminiscent of the Depression era, gave the office a funereal appearance. The setting was accentuated by framed prints, evenly spaced on the hallway walls, depicting scenes from nineteenth-century courts in England, and long-forgotten, portly jurists with enormous jowls and powdered wigs wearing expressions of smug self-importance.

    The stodgy atmosphere of the décor was quickly swept aside by the vigor of the lawyers who occupied the suite of offices. But there is always the exception to the rule. In this case, the exception was older than the other lawyers, heavy-set, bald, with a round face, bulbous nose and enormous jowls. He shuffled slightly as he walked. Except for his dark blue suit and tie, he looked just like the English jurists in the framed prints hanging on the walls. He was not identified with any particular department or specialty. He had no position of management or authority. He seemed to be a man who did not fit in. His name was Frank B. Murdoch.

    The workload for a new lawyer at that firm was staggering. Often it required travel to distant cities for weeks at a time. Even when travel was not required, the work consumed virtually every minute of the available time. One's attention was constantly focused on files and deadlines. It was like *One Day in the Life of Ivan Denisovich*, but set in a law firm. I was surprised one morning when I answered the

Frank B. Murdoch and Catherine St. John

phone and heard a voice say, "This is Frank Murdoch." Why would he be calling me? He was not involved in any of the cases on which I was working.

Murdoch said he and his wife would like to invite my wife, Cathy, and me, along with several other lawyers to dinner and then to hear the orchestra at Robin Hood Dell. It was a nice invitation but I was scheduled to be out of town on that date so the invitation was declined. Nonetheless, I wondered what the evening would have been like and whether we would have had anything in common. I need not have wondered.

A few months later, Ed Mullinix called and asked me to help Frank Murdoch with a new matter that was coming into the firm later that day. At precisely 4:30 p.m. that afternoon, three men arrived at the office. One was the president and another the vice president of a California business school. The third was their lawyer, a sole practitioner who also happened to be the brother-in-law of the president. He had no litigation experience. They were in town for an arbitration in which the school was accused of securities fraud, involving a claim for $2.2 million. Apparently, they arrived at the hearing with the expectation that it would be a discussion session and nothing more. Their expectation was incorrect. The arbitrators expected the parties to go forward with the presentation of testimony. The chairman of the arbitration panel, a prominent Philadelphia lawyer, strongly suggested they retain competent local counsel. He then postponed the hearing for forty-five days but required that the business school file with the arbitrators the next day a detailed statement of its legal position.

We escorted the visitors to a conference room where we discussed the general nature of the representation. I was impressed by Murdoch's comfortable manner of speaking to three strangers. I had not previously noticed his facial expression of mixed curiosity and amusement, like a child looking at a new toy. He took a yellow legal pad and elaborately recorded the name, address and telephone number of each of the people at the table and the name and address of the business school. He also said we would take care of the filing the next day and inquired as to the details of the claim and the availability of the school's files. The president reached into his briefcase and produced a substantial set of files. He said he could explain them. At that point, Frank B. Murdoch looked at his watch, apologized for having to leave for a previous appointment, but he reassured the new clients that "Mr. St. John will take care of everything." The image of Frank Murdoch walking out that door is indelibly impressed in my memory.

We worked on that case for about six months. By the time it ended, I had a completely different view of Frank Murdoch. Frank Murdoch was an upbeat person who could find something interesting in almost any circumstance, and who could laugh at himself in the face of adversity. At the drop of a hat, he would regale anyone who would listen with tales of his past experiences.

Frank was raised in the rowhouse neighborhoods of West Philadelphia. Like many youngsters, he had a paper route. But Frank did not stop with just one. When another route became available, he signed up for that one, too.

Recognizing that he did not have the time to serve two routes, he recruited one of his friends to handle the second route with the understanding that Frank would do all of the collections and would receive twenty-five percent of the income. Pretty soon he had four or five routes that were served by four or five boys who, in effect, worked for Frank, who worked only one day each week collecting from the customers. In the meanwhile, he would use his wagon to collect wood that was placed out for trash collection. Murdoch's father would boast to his neighbors that he rarely had to purchase coal to heat the house because the basement was usually stocked from floor to ceiling with the firewood that young Frank had collected.

The street-smart Murdoch put himself through the University of Pennsylvania and its law school. His graduation from law school in 1929 coincided almost exactly with the onset of the Great Depression. The graduates who were at the very top of their class found jobs. The rest, including Frank Murdoch, had to shift for themselves. It was tough for a young lawyer to scratch out a living when so many businesses were shutting down.

One afternoon, Frank was commiserating with the landlord of the building in which he rented an office. The landlord complained about the Depression having caused a sharp decrease in rental income but no decrease in expenses, including real estate taxes. Frank had an idea! He would represent the landlord in an action to reduce the tax assessment, and his fee would be a small percentage of any saving that was achieved. The landlord agreed. Frank then went to the library to determine how to go about getting a tax assessment reduced. He filed the appropriate papers and was successful. The landlord was ecstatic.

Pretty soon many of the center city banks were asking their lawyers about reducing their real estate assessments.

The major law firms in those days considered municipal tax assessments to be a grubby sort of work that was done by less-prestigious lawyers. They were not inclined to lower themselves into that type of work for what they thought would be a single case for a single client. Thus, the big law firms referred their clients to that nice young fellow who specialized in reducing tax assessments. In no time at all, Frank Murdoch's list of clients included most of Philadelphia's major banks and insurance companies. Three years into the Depression, Murdoch was able to afford a chauffeur and lived in a mansion that he rented in Andalusia.

Murdoch's star was in the ascendant. He joined with several powerful lawyers to start a major law firm, Bell, Murdoch & Paxson, with offices in the prestigious Fidelity Building on South Broad Street, across from The Union League. Frank was also a significant force in the Republican Party, which controlled both the Philadelphia and Pennsylvania governments. But things were about to change. Frank's ability to deal with adversity was about to be tested to an almost unprecedented extent.

It began with his law firm, then known as Bell, Murdoch, Paxson & Dilworth. After World War II, name partner Richardson Dilworth returned from service with the Marine Corps and took a leadership role in the firm. Dilworth was becoming a leader in the Democratic Party and was intent on wresting political control of Philadelphia from the Republicans. The conflict between the patrician Dilworth and the earthy Murdoch was irreconcilable. The firm was not big enough for the both of them, and Murdoch was forced out in 1948.

Murdoch's Republican Party connections came to the rescue. William A. Schnader, long a stalwart of the Republican Party in Pennsylvania, offered Murdoch a place in the Schnader firm. Although Schnader's hard-driving, workaholic dedication to the law was in sharp contrast to the gregarious lifestyle of Frank Murdoch, the expectation was that this would not be a long-term relationship. It was a presidential year, and the polls showed that the Republican Party's candidate was a virtual certainty to be elected in November.

Murdoch was the Pennsylvania chairman for the Republican presidential candidate. A reliable rumor was that a pre-election meeting of the party's leaders had been held to discuss presidential appointments and that the competition was most heated for the posts of attorney general and secretary of state. At one point, someone turned to Murdoch and said, "How about you, Frank, what do you want?" Frank smiled and looked slowly around the room at the politicians who were now competing against each other for the choice appointments. With an amused expression he said, "What about solicitor general?" It is probable that no one in that room had any idea what a solicitor general did but they knew instinctively that Frank was not competing with them for the most desirable assignments. They unanimously agreed that Frank B. Murdoch would be solicitor general in the cabinet of President Thomas E. Dewey.

Of course, the 1948 presidential election is now history, ancient history to most. It was, perhaps, the greatest upset in any United States presidential election and is best portrayed by the photograph of a grinning President Harry S. Truman holding aloft a newspaper that had been published early in the post-election day morning with a premature headline boldly proclaiming, "DEWEY WINS!" That photograph captures the irony and the joy of victory. But it is not hard to imagine the shock and the heartbreak of defeat, particularly for those who had worked hard on the election campaign and who were looking forward to positions of high office. But Frank Murdoch did not sulk. He reveled in telling the story to anyone who would listen.

The Republicans had planned an elaborate victory party at the Bellevue Stratford Hotel. It would begin late in the evening after the polls had closed and while the returns were being counted. Frank was in his hotel room trying to fix the studs on his formal dress shirt. He turned on a radio to catch the early election returns. "I heard the announcer's voice droning in the background and stopped fooling with the shirt studs. I went closer to the radio and listened for a few minutes. Then I went and knocked on Marguerite's door and said, 'No need to rush dear. Take your time.'" By this point, Frank's body would be shaking with laughter at the memory of the fading dream.

The disappointments of depressions, politics and law practices were just a part of the total experience. Frank and his wife, Marguerite, had three sons. Graeme Murdoch was the only son to become a lawyer. For a time, Graeme was an assistant U.S. Attorney. One evening in the 1960s, after dropping off his date in town, Graeme was driving home when he became confused as he passed a highway construction site. He swung his sports car into an access lane that was barricaded by a cyclone fence and other construction material. There was a terrible accident. A fence pole went into Graeme's head, destroying part of his brain. The brain damage was permanent. Graeme survived but it was expected that he would be non-responsive — as most people put it, "a vegetable."

It took a few years, but the financial burden of Graeme's medical care was resolved when Gerry Litvin, whom Frank had retained to bring a negligence action on behalf of Graeme, obtained a $3 million verdict against the City of Philadelphia, the highest award of its kind at that time. But Frank Murdoch was not satisfied simply to make the financial arrangements for Graeme and to defer to the medical personnel. As soon as Graeme's condition became more stable, Murdoch began to include Graeme in his social events.

Murdoch had excellent taste in entertaining. He hosted dinner parties at The Union League, particularly when there was musical entertainment such as one of the military service academy choruses or the Wiffenpoofs. The Philadelphia Country Club was a regular stop when it was elaborately decorated for Christmas and Easter. On most occasions, Frank Murdoch consciously invited a number of men and women who were close to the same age as Graeme. He thought that Graeme would benefit by being in the company of his contemporaries.

It is hard to say whether Graeme Murdoch's well-being was materially advanced by being in close proximity to people his own age. But it is beyond any doubt that his progress was amazing. When I first met Graeme, a medical attendant was always at his side, ready to assist if he stumbled or fell. Graeme would look at you but was unable to speak, much like the victim of a severe stroke. Gradually, the medical attendant was not needed. Still later, Graeme began to speak in a low, halting voiced. He spoke short sentences or, sometimes, just basic thoughts. But this was a man who was supposed to be a vegetable, unable to walk, talk or even think. The medical explanation was that a normally dormant lobe of the brain became activated and replaced some of the functions that had been destroyed.

I last saw Graeme at a dinner party at the Philadelphia Country Club. After dinner, we were seated in the lounge area and an exuberant Frank Murdoch announced that he was going to take some of his guests on a short tour of the club. I was sitting next to Graeme. As Frank Murdoch led the group across the lounge, Graeme watched and then turned to me and said, "He's quite a guy." Indeed he was.

Frank B. Murdoch died July 19, 1982 at the age of 79. His son Graeme died in 1998, at the age of 68, thirty-five years after his terrible accident.

BARNEY SMOLENS:
A Reminiscence

©Philadelphia Bar Association, reprinted with permission

In the 1960s, most law schools did not teach trial advocacy. Accordingly, one of the first challenges facing a recent law school graduate was to find an experienced lawyer who would not mind having a youngster tag along through the course of a trial. It occurred to me that Barney Smolens might be that kind of experienced lawyer.

Bernard J. Smolens was then in his mid-fifties. A short, slender, gray-haired man with a pixie-ish sense of humor, he had a strong background in personal injury defense and general commercial trial practice. In the Schnader law firm, Barney was one of the lawyers who handled the defense of cases brought against Yellow Cab Company of Philadelphia. He was also a fun-loving man who welcomed the company of young lawyers at the regular Monday night dinners at T'arellos and lunches at the Vesper Club. I knew that Barney was getting ready for the trial of a Yellow Cab case. His reaction was exactly what I had hoped it would be. He said that he would be delighted to have me sit in with him during the trial. The case was *Lacey v. Yellow Cab Company*.

Gus Lacey was a familiar name in Philadelphia in the 1960s. An African American, Gus was a handsome man. His pencil-thin moustache fit in perfectly with his square jaw and trim figure. As a young man, he sold lingerie door-to-door in the rowhouse neighborhoods. The good-looking, smooth-talking Lacey was very successful at what he did. And in the process, he became known as "Mr. Silk." Later, he bought the spacious bar at the corner of 52nd and Spruce Streets and named the business "Mr. Silk's Third Base." Gus' motto was, "You have to touch Third Base before you go home."

The accident happened shortly before midnight. Gus Lacey was a passenger in a Yellow Cab. He was returning to Mr. Silk's to supervise the closing of the bar and the preparation for the following day's activities. At the intersection of 52nd and Chestnut Streets, the cab was hit by a car that was traveling east on Chestnut. Gus suffered what people usually call a "whiplash" injury. Suit was filed against the driver of the other car and against the cab company. The cab driver was one of the company's old-timers, an excellent driver who wore a uniform and considered himself to be a professional.

Deposition testimony was taken and Gus Lacey supported the cab driver, saying that the traffic light was green for traffic moving on 52nd Street. After the deposition was taken, it was determined that the other car had no insurance. If Lacey was to collect any money from his lawsuit, it would have to be paid by Yellow Cab and that would require a finding that the cab driver was negligent. Yellow Cab's claims people were convinced that Gus Lacey could not credibly attack the cab driver in light of his deposition testimony. Yellow Cab expected Barney Smolens to use Lacey's own deposition testimony to destroy him on cross-examination.

Barney's background as a defense lawyer was evident from the mementos that cluttered his office. His favorite was the old-fashioned cab meter on the windowsill behind his desk. When one of the firm's associates wanted his opinion, Barney would ceremoniously put his feet up on the edge of the desk, lean back in his chair and, with an exaggerated sweep of his left hand, bang the meter flag to the "down" position. As the loud tick-tock filled the room, Barney would say, "Well, go ahead m'boy. Ask your question; the meter's

144

running." He loved posturing, striking dramatic poses and delivering his comments with theatrical timing. When speaking, he delighted in the use of grammatically incorrect words and malapropism. He would begin a sentence with the word "irregardless" and then pause as if hanging the word out to dry before continuing with his thought. In place of "rapport" he would say "rappaport," the surname of the well-known real estate speculator, Samuel Rappaport. And he was always ready with a funny story or the very latest joke.

During World War II, Barney was a waist gunner on a B-17 bomber based in England. The plane was shot down while on a bombing run over the Baltic. The crew bailed out. Barney was taken prisoner. He spent the next year-and-a-half in a German prison camp. To hear Barney talk about this experience, you almost began to think that he did it deliberately to gather background material for humorous stories. He said that he was the most literary-minded of the prisoners in his stalag. Pretty soon, the other POWs sought out Barney to write letters for them to girlfriends, wives and family members. He was paid with cigarettes, which were highly valued in the prison camp. Often he found himself orchestrating long-distance romances, the stockade's version of Cyrano de Bergerac. And then there was the time that the men in his barracks collected whatever chocolate they could get, whether it be

145

from Red Cross packages of cocoa or packages from home. After months of collecting, they pooled their resources and baked a chocolate cake in a C-ration tin can on the potbellied coal stove. He described something that looked like three hockey pucks stacked one on top of the other. They cut it into sixteen pieces. Barney said it was the best cake he ever tasted.

The case of *Lacey v. Yellow Cab Company* was called for trial in City Hall before Judge Theodore Gutowicz, sitting without a jury. During recesses in the trial, Gus Lacey would invariably walk over to our table and trade jokes with Barney.

Finally, the time came for Gus Lacey to testify about the accident. As we expected, Gus now said that he "thought that the light was *red* for the Yellow Cab." A witness who contradicts his own deposition testimony is a sitting duck for cross-examination. There is a tendency on the part of the witness to try to explain away the inconsistency. But it is almost impossible to wiggle out of the contradiction. The inevitable result is the repetition and re-repetition of the deposition testimony, to the point where the attempted explanation makes no sense at all.

Standing at the counsel table, Barney picked up the deposition transcript with his left hand, and with his right hand, flicked open his reading glasses. He quickly found the page that he wanted. Leaning forward over the table, he said, "Now, Mr. Lacey, do you recall what you said about the traffic light when you testified under oath just six months after the accident?" When Gus answered in the negative, Barney held up the transcript, pointed to the page and said, "Right here at page 79, line 14, you testified that, Quote, 'The light on 52nd Street was *green*,' Unquote." Dramatically whipping the reading glasses from the bridge of his nose, Barney demanded, "What do you say about that?" Gus looked Barney straight in the eye; his expression showing only amused curiosity. Slowly, his smile became wider, almost as though Barney had told a joke, and in a cool, clear voice Gus said, "Well, how about that?" In a twinkling, Barney's fish slipped off the hook. Later that afternoon, the case was settled.

      A few weeks after the trial, I stopped by Barney's office to ask him a question. Before I could say a word, he flashed a big smile and said, "Guess who I just talked to on the telephone?" Answering his own question, he added, "Gus Lacey!" Barney said that Gus chatted for a while and then invited Barney to come out and have a martini on the house at Mr. Silk's Third Base. When Barney declined, Gus sensed the reason. Gus told him that he had nothing to worry about: that Gus would have one of "his boys" pick up Barney at the office and drive him back to the office after they finished their drink. Barney was obviously delighted by the offer but still he declined. Perhaps he was worried about how he would explain it to the people at Yellow Cab Company.

      Over the years, I learned a lot from Barney Smolens. We tried several cases together and collaborated on a number of others. To a great extent, trial lawyering is an exercise in decision-making; and Barney and I sometimes advocated divergent courses of action. It wasn't often that I disagreed with Barney. Reasonable men do differ on occasion, however, and one such disagreement dates back to the days of Mr. Silk. Contrary to the best judgment of my friend Barney, I would have been inclined to touch Third Base before going home.

III. PHILADELPHIA BAR HISTORY

Before The Philadelphia Bar Association celebrated its bicentennial in 2002, I was asked to write a short history of the bar association. It was a lengthy undertaking that required several years of spare-time research. Very few practicing lawyers on the bicentennial committee had any idea of the exploits of their predecessors.

In the final analysis, I fudged the result. I wrote about the bar association, but the focus of my writing was on the Philadelphia lawyers, regardless of whether or not they were members of the bar association.

That bicentennial research provided the basis for the following articles, all of which were published in the Philadelphia Lawyer Magazine.

JAMES WILSON:

A Forgotten Father

©Philadelphia Bar Association, reprinted with permission

On August 21, 1798, a reclusive old man was found dead in his room at Horniblow's Tavern, in the tiny tidewater town of Edenton, North Carolina. He was gaunt. His clothes were ill-fitting and stained. He was a man on the run, a fugitive trying to elude a swarm of creditors. Twice he had been jailed, most recently on the complaint of Pierce Butler, the influential senator from South Carolina. He needed a place to hide, but where? Who could he trust? Stress became depression. Malaria set in, and finally there was a stroke. He looked much older than his 56 years. But this man was no derelict. He was an associate justice of the Supreme Court of the United States; he was a Philadelphia lawyer; he signed the Declaration of Independence; and he was a key figure in making the Constitution of the United States. He was James Wilson, a "founding father."

Born in the Scottish Lowlands, Wilson always seemed to be short of money. His parents sacrificed the few possessions that they had to finance his education for the ministry. It was a first rate education that included studies at the universities of St. Andrews and Edinburgh. But Wilson was not inclined toward the ministry. Instead, he borrowed money to emigrate to America. In Philadelphia, he found a job teaching at what is now the University of Pennsylvania. The job did not pay very much. Again he borrowed money, this time to pay for the privilege of reading the law in John Dickinson's law office. Dickinson was a scholar and a patriot, the author of the influential *Letters of a Pennsylvania Farmer*.

Upon his admission to the bar in 1766, Wilson found himself unable to compete with established lawyers for the representation of "Old Philadelphia" clients. He headed west; first to Reading and then to Carlisle which, at that time, was the outer edge of the untamed frontier. He was a forceful advocate for the rough-and-tumble frontiersmen. As he rode the circuit of courts in Lancaster, Reading and Carlisle, Wilson began to acquire real estate. He borrowed the money necessary to make those purchases. In 1778, Wilson moved back to Philadelphia where he joined with other like-minded property owners to form a commercial bank. The banking enterprise was followed by the acquisition of speculative real estate in New York, Virginia, the Carolinas, Georgia and the western territory. Extensive land holdings along the Lackawaxen River in northeast Pennsylvania, known as "Wilsonville," were being developed for metal working and textile industries. It was a vast empire; and it gave the impression of immense wealth. But appearances were deceiving. The empire was constructed with borrowed money; and it was stretched to the breaking point.

Wilson was a formidable trial lawyer. His courtroom skills were valued by his Carlisle clients. But those self-sufficient frontiersmen were increasingly upset by Wilson's actions as their representative in the Continental Congress. It was his position in congress that gave Wilson the opportunity to sign the Declaration of Independence. Wilson labored as a legislator. He was frequently frustrated by the inability of the confederation to take concerted action and even to pay and equip the soldiers who were fighting a difficult war. Nonetheless, Wilson persisted in his legislative duties, all the while studying governmental theory, searching for a means to improve the machinery of government.

After his return to Philadelphia, the scope of Wilson's law practice expanded beyond property claims. He now handled admiralty disputes and criminal defense cases, often representing well-to-do Quaker businessmen accused of consorting with the enemy during the British occupation. Wilson's outspoken dislike for the Articles of Confederation, coupled with his unpopular defense of "traitors," angered many people. At one point, a group of thirty or more armed militiamen took things into their own hands and attacked Wilson's house at Third and Walnut Streets. Five men were killed and seventeen were wounded in the firefight at the house that Philadelphians would later call "Fort Wilson."

When he was chosen to be a delegate to the convention that was called to propose improvements to the Articles of Confederation, Wilson's place in history was assured. Wilson's long service in the congress convinced him of the need for a strong central government, capable of raising funds sufficient to support itself. His wide-ranging practice of law convinced him of the need for a strong and independent judiciary, a judiciary that would determine the supreme law of the land. His intellectual study of government gave him a solid foundation for the task. And his experience as a trial lawyer gave him the ability to advocate those objectives in a forceful and effective manner.

The 55 delegates who met in Philadelphia in May 1787 brought with them not only their collective wisdom but also their individual weaknesses and self-interests. Prominent among those personal agendas were the power considerations that pitted small states against large states, and sovereign states against a strong national government. The concept of sovereignty demanded that there be only one sovereign, one supreme authority. If sovereignty was vested in the states, then by definition the national government could not be sovereign, and vice versa. The convention nearly ground to a halt on issues of state and federal sovereignty.

Wilson took the lead in resolving this thorny issue. His biographer, Charles Page Smith, concludes that "Wilson did more than any other man in the convention, Madison included, to enunciate the rather novel theory that both state and national government might be supreme within their respective orbits – that sovereignty might indeed be divided." Wilson's view was that government arose from the collective will of the people. From that proposition, it followed not only that the people could vest power in both a state and a national government, but also that government at every level should be determined by the will of the people.

Consistent with this basic principle, Wilson forcefully advocated the interests of the people. He was successful in achieving a lower house of congress that would be elected by the people. On the other hand, he was not able to persuade his fellow delegates to allow the direct election of senators. It was in the self-interest of those delegates that senators be elected by representatives such as themselves. One hundred and twenty-six years later, in 1913, the Seventeenth Amendment would be ratified, putting into effect the direct election of senators that Wilson had advocated from the beginning. Wilson was partially successful effecting his proposal that the president be elected by the people rather than by congress. A compromise was worked out and a system of presidential electors resulted in an indirect election by the people.

Finally, Wilson did succeed in his efforts to establish a strong and independent judiciary, defeating the efforts of those delegates who wanted to make the judiciary subordinate to congress. The judicial structure of a Supreme Court as the highest authority in the land, and the appointment of judges by the president are also ideas championed by Wilson.

In the years following the adoption of the constitution, whenever the delegates were asked to identify the most influential persons at the convention, James Wilson was always among those mentioned. Even today, when historians and other scholars identify the most influential delegates of the Constitutional Convention, James Wilson is always among the names – usually listed second only to James Madison. His convention colleague Dr. Benjamin Rush described Wilson's mind as "one blaze of light." Nonetheless, as Catherine Drinker Bowen noted in her story of the Constitutional Convention, *Miracle at Philadelphia*, "Wilson has not been much described by historians."

Why historians have not much described Wilson is difficult to explain. The breadth of his achievements was matched by few of his contemporaries. In addition to his participation in the Declaration of Independence and the Constitutional Convention, Wilson took the lead in drafting the Constitution of Pennsylvania in 1790. In December of that year, Wilson began a series of four lectures on law at the College of Philadelphia. Today, the University of Pennsylvania traces the roots of its law school to Wilson's lectures. Wilson was the fourth person appointed to the Supreme Court of the United States by President George Washington. As a member of the original Supreme Court, Wilson participated in the important cases of first impression upon which the power of the judiciary developed.

Wilson was an outstanding lawyer, an effective advocate. He had a great intellect. He did not hesitate to represent unpopular causes. He accomplished his successes without the benefit of wealth or social contacts. However, there was also much to dislike about James Wilson. A single-minded advocate, he could alienate his opponents to the point of violence. His participation in real estate and business schemes was compulsive – bordering on addiction – and it subjected him to accusations of avarice.

James Wilson was a complex man. Viewed in retrospect, it appears as though Wilson's life was designed for one very specific purpose. The years of preparation – the advocacy of rugged American frontiersmen, the dreadful hours devoted to an ineffective Continental Congress, the embarrassment of a nation unable to support its patriotic army, the ineffectiveness of the confederated judicial system – it all came together in four short months in 1787, when James Wilson was a driving force of the convention that produced the Constitution of the United States. For that enduring achievement, James Wilson should live in our memory.

In 1798, it was difficult for Wilson to live anywhere. The cold winds of economic depression tore his paper empire to shreds. As he rode the circuits assigned to members of the Supreme Court, Wilson was ever conscious of the possibility of imprisonment. A creditor caught up with him in Burlington, New Jersey, and he was thrown in jail until he could raise the amount of three hundred dollars. Upon his release from the Burlington jail, he traveled south. Judge James Iredell (pronounced "ire-dell"), a colleague on the bench of the Supreme Court, suggested that Wilson might find refuge in Iredell's hometown of Edenton, North Carolina. Even there, he was discovered and jailed, this time by Pierce Butler who had represented South Carolina at the Constitutional Convention a decade earlier. Butler held a substantial note that had been co-signed by Wilson. When the end finally came, Judge Iredell saw to it that Wilson was buried in the family burial plot of Iredell's father-in-law, at Hayes Plantation, on the south side of Queen Anne Creek, outside Edenton. Wilson was quickly forgotten.

In 1906, President Theodore Roosevelt sparked renewed interest in Wilson. During the dedication of Pennsylvania's new capitol building in Harrisburg, Roosevelt singled out Wilson for special praise. Roosevelt saw in Wilson's constitutional experience the philosophical roots of his own Progressive Movement. One month after the Harrisburg speech, Wilson's remains were removed from Hayes Plantation and reinterred at Old Christ Church in Philadelphia. But Roosevelt's praise also triggered a hostile reaction by opponents of the Roosevelt Administration – mainly big businesses and the corporate lawyers who represented them (the Chancellor of the Bar Association included) – who feared that a surge of interest in Wilson might generate increased public support for Roosevelt's efforts to regulate private enterprise. Again, James Wilson lapsed into relative obscurity; even the marker on his grave states the wrong date. Ironically, his final resting place is just a short walk from the grave of his creditor, South Carolina's Pierce Butler.

PETER STEPHEN DU PONCEAU:

A Man of Letters

© Philadelphia Bar Association, Reprinted with permission

"Nobody knows the trouble I've seen." It is the opening line of a well-known spiritual. This statement might also apply to lawyers, who are bound to maintain the confidentiality of their clients' affairs and, accordingly, cannot share many of their troubles with colleagues or friends. Perhaps that is why almost all of the entertaining books about lawyers are works of fiction, for example, *Anatomy of a Murder*, *To Kill a Mockingbird*, and *The Philadelphian*. The dearth of interesting biographies, particularly autobiographies, about lawyers might also be due to the fact that lawyers are used to writing about or on behalf of others; we somehow feel uneasy when it comes to writing about ourselves. And the inevitable result is that many outstanding lawyers are soon forgotten. Such is the case with Peter Stephen Du Ponceau.

In 1802, Du Ponceau was one of the seventy-one lawyers who founded what is now called the Philadelphia Bar Association. He was 42 years of age and an accomplished lawyer. He was recognized as an expert in the law relating to international commercial transactions. He was fluent in virtually all of the European languages. He handled cases arising from significant events of his time. For example, in *McIlvaine v Coxe*, 4 Cranch 209 (1808), Du Ponceau argued that a resident of New Jersey who left the country shortly after the Declaration of Independence and who had declared his allegiance to Britain should be considered an alien who forfeited his title to real estate in the United States. Du

Ponceau also represented European merchants whose cargoes had been seized or destroyed on the high seas. Along with his Philadelphia lawyer colleagues, William Lewis, Alexander Dallas, Jared Ingersoll, William Rawle and Edward Tilghman, Du Ponceau annually made the three-day journey in February to appear in the Supreme Court in Washington, D.C.

Moreover, Du Ponceau was not a one-dimensional person, not by any stretch of the imagination. He served as president of the American Philosophical Society, the organization founded by Benjamin Franklin for the advancement of science. President Thomas Jefferson wanted to appoint Du Ponceau Chief Justice of Louisiana. Du Ponceau declined the appointment. He was the second Chancellor of the Philadelphia Bar Association, and the first provost of The Law Academy. He was president of the Historical Society of Pennsylvania. And he received high praise, including an international award, for his treatise on the grammatical structure of the languages of Indians in North America. His work on the languages of North American Indians drew the attention of Alexis de Tocqueville who was gathering information for his classic *Democracy in America*. Tocqueville made it a point to interview Peter Du Ponceau.

But a recitation of one's accomplishments, viewed in isolation, tells us little about the man and his times. In early nineteenth century Philadelphia, nearly everyone urged Du Ponceau to write an autobiography. Yet, Du Ponceau demurred. He did not seek public attention. He could not understand why anyone would find the story of his life to be of any significance.

In 1836, there was a change. After the death of William Rawle, Philadelphia lawyer Thomas I. Wharton undertook to write a memoir on Rawle. Wharton asked for Du Ponceau's help. Wharton asked the 76-year old Du Ponceau to write a letter containing his recollections of Rawle. Du Ponceau wrote the letter; and it contained as much about the world of Peter Du Ponceau as it did about his friend William Rawle.

Du Ponceau told about William Lewis, the Philadelphia lawyer with whom he studied the law in 1784. Lewis was the son of a Chester County farmer. As a youth, Lewis would bring his father's horse and wagon to the market in Philadelphia. After selling the vegetables, Lewis would go into the courthouse at Second and Market Streets and listen to the lawyers. This sparked a keen interest in the legal profession. Lewis sought an apprenticeship with lawyer George Ross, and was eventually admitted to the bar. Du Ponceau's letter describes Lewis as, "at that time [1784] the most celebrated lawyer in Philadelphia, and, perhaps, in the United States."

It was while studying with Lewis that Du Ponceau met Rawle. Du Ponceau and Rawle had a mutual interest in law books. And in 1785, Rawle was one of the two examiners who interviewed Du Ponceau for admission to the bar of the Philadelphia Court of Common Pleas.

Du Ponceau's letter describes his February journeys with Messrs. Lewis, Dallas, Ingersoll, Rawle and Tilghman to the Supreme Court of the United States. Those six Philadelphia lawyers shared a stagecoach and also shared the bumps and bruises inflicted by three days travel in each direction, much of it over rugged forest roads. How did those preeminent Philadelphia lawyers conduct themselves on their way to the highest court in the land? Du Ponceau's letter tells us that "as soon as we were out of the city, and felt the flush of air, we were like school boys on the play ground on a holiday; and we began to kill time by all the means that our imagination could suggest." They sang, made outrageous puns, told jokes and generally made fun of each other.

In February 1808, after Rawle and Du Ponceau had argued opposite sides of the *McIlvaine* case, their courtroom argument was resumed in the stagecoach on the way back to Philadelphia. Rawle had argued in court that, although the British subject had sworn allegiance to Britain, the revolution acted as a new birth and that he became a citizen, albeit against his own will. Du Ponceau had responded that he had "never heard of a surgical operation, by which the subject was extracted from the womb, with the revolutionary *forceps*." Sharp comments about "forceps" flashed back and forth among the six passengers. The driver was so caught up in the quick exchanges of wit that he failed to see a tree stump in the road. The coach nearly overturned. The driver was thrown from his seat and the horses ran uncontrolled toward a dangerous bridge across a river. All six lawyers leaped from the hurtling stagecoach and went sprawling across the Maryland countryside. Had it not been for an honest and resourceful farmer who later found and returned the horses and stage, it would have been a long walk to Baltimore.

Du Ponceau's letter makes it clear that a strong camaraderie developed among those six lawyers. They not only traveled to the Supreme Court as a unit but they also arrived at court together and they left together. And Justice Bushrod Washington, who had read the law in Philadelphia, welcomed them with the proud declaration, "This is *my* bar."

Du Ponceau may have doubted his own ability to write an autobiography but his letter to Wharton provides an interesting snapshot of Philadelphia lawyers in the early 1800's. And this was not the only letter of that type that Du Ponceau wrote. In 1836, Robert Walsh, a journalist, asked Du Ponceau to write a series of letters about his life. Over the next year, Du Ponceau wrote seven letters to Walsh. But then Walsh moved to Paris and the project was abandoned. About one year later, Du Ponceau's granddaughter, Anna Garesché, persuaded him to resume writing the autobiographical letters. Reluctantly, Du Ponceau acquiesced and continued the course of letters even though his health was declining. The last several letters were dictated by Du Ponceau to Anna; who wrote them out in longhand. The letters describe the early life of Peter S. Du Ponceau. And a fascinating life it was.

Du Ponceau was born on the Isle of Re, just off the coast of France, in the Bay of Biscay. His mother wanted him to become a priest. His father, an army officer, wanted him to join the military – that is, until it was determined that "Pierre" was very nearsighted. Peter did not want to become a soldier. But he did enjoy being at the garrison on the Isle of Re where he came into contact with military men from many countries. Peter was gifted when it came to languages. He would talk to the foreign soldiers; and before long, he would be speaking that soldier's native language. Peter also did not want to be a priest. At the age of 13 years, his mother enrolled Peter in a college of Benedictine monks, and two years later, in the abbey at La Rochelle to study for the priesthood. One month after entering the abbey, Peter ran away to Paris where he supported himself by translating English writings, later taking a position as secretary to a minister who was engaged in literary efforts. It was not long before he met an unemployed Prussian soldier, Captain Frederick Steuben.

Most Americans are familiar with the story of Steuben – how Benjamin Franklin in France feared that the Continental Congress would ignore this Prussian captain; how Franklin wrote a letter introducing Steuben as "Baron de Steuben, lately a lieutenant-general in the king of Prussia's service;" and how Baron Von Steuben instilled discipline in the ragged American army at Valley Forge. What is usually left out of the story is that Steuben spoke little or no English. All of Steuben's commands and his training manual were written by his 17-year old secretary, who then held the rank of captain, Peter Du Ponceau. It was not exactly the military career that his father had in mind. But at the early age of 17 years, Peter Du Ponceau found himself an officer on the staff of General George Washington, a staff that included Alexander Hamilton, Aaron Burr, John Marshall, James Monroe and the Marquis de Lafayette, among others.

Over the next two years, Du Ponceau was promoted to the rank of major. He participated in cavalry sorties as far north as West Point and New Rochelle. When Steuben was ordered south, Du Ponceau went with him to Virginia where they were engaged in a series of minor frays with the cavalry of Lord Cornwallis. It was in 1779 that Du Ponceau was first diagnosed as suffering from "consumption," a broad term typically applied to tuberculosis and similar diseases. Still, Du Ponceau continued with the army as far south as the North Carolina border. At that point, illness forced him to turn back and return to Philadelphia. Everyone thought that Du Ponceau was going to die.

Du Ponceau did not die – at least at that time. In Philadelphia, his health gradually improved. In 1782, with the help of Steuben's recommendation and the influence of other significant leaders, he obtained employment in the Office of Foreign Affairs, which was headed by Robert Livingston. It was a logical step from the Office of Foreign Affairs to the law office of William Lewis. However, it is at this point that the letters stopped.

Peter Stephen Du Ponceau died on April 1, 1844. Before he died, he expressed regret that he had not begun writing his letters earlier in life. Had he written more letters, Peter Du Ponceau might be a familiar figure. Instead, Du Ponceau has been treated by history as a person to be dismissed summarily with adjectival characterizations that are often inconsistent, *e.g.*, "an upper class Philadelphian," "specifically *not* an Old Philadelphian," and "a French auslander." On the other hand, Philadelphia lawyers should be grateful for the letters that were written and the insights that those letters preserved. Moreover, it is entirely appropriate that the new building on Independence Mall places the Liberty Bell almost exactly on the site of Du Ponceau's home and law office.

OWEN WISTER:
WHEN YOU CALL ME THAT, SMILE!
©*Philadelphia Bar Association, reprinted with permission*

Medicine Bow, Wyoming is just a speck on the Rocky Mountain plains. It has only 274 residents. Cattlemen no longer bring their livestock to Medicine Bow for shipment by rail. Cattle are now shipped by truck directly from the ranch. The railroad tracks still run through Medicine Bow. But the trains no longer stop. Instead, each train, as it rumbles by, blasts a high-decibel salute on its pneumatic horn. The fabled "Lincoln Highway" still runs through Medicine Bow. But motor vehicles no longer use the old Route 30. Motor vehicles today use the limited-access interstate highway I-80. Where the lonesome Lincoln Highway passes the south edge of Medicine Bow, there is a pyramid-shaped mound of petrified wood, about seven feet high. It is an unlikely place to find a monument to a Philadelphia lawyer. The monument is for Owen Wister, the man who put Medicine Bow on the map.

In 1902, as the Philadelphia Bar Association celebrated its centennial anniversary, Philadelphia lawyer Owen Wister published the world's first cowboy novel, *The*

Virginian. Wister's story begins in Medicine Bow. In fact, Medicine Bow is the only town specifically identified. The novel centers on a self-reliant cowboy known by his place of origin as "the Virginian." Wister's novel established a pattern for virtually all of the thousands of cowboy stories that followed. The Virginian has continuing clashes with a villainous cowhand who is set on destroying the highly ethical hero. There is also a subplot involving the Virginian's romantic interest in a schoolteacher who had been raised in a very proper family in the East. At the climax, there is a shoot-out between the Virginian and the villain.

The most memorable scene occurs in a Medicine Bow saloon. The villain, anxious to get on with a poker game, addresses the Virginian as "you son-of-a-bitch." In response, the Virginian draws his six-shooter, rests his gun-hand easily on the table, and says, "When you call me that, *smile*!"

The Virginian was a huge success. It was republished more than fifty times and sold millions of copies. Five times it was made into a movie; two were silent films. The first of the "sound" movies featured a young actor named Gary Cooper and launched him on his way to stardom. *The Virginian* was also produced as a stage show and later as a television series. It established Owen Wister's reputation as a first-rate novelist.

Owen Wister was one of the "Germantown" Wisters whose forbears immigrated to America from Heidelberg in the early 1700's. They established an import business, and married into the prosperous Logan and Fisher families. On his mother's side, Owen was descended from the world-famous actress Fanny Kemble, and from Pierce Butler, who represented South Carolina at the Constitutional Convention of 1787. The family home, "Butler Place," was located the Ogontz section of Philadelphia. Wister's family pedigree was pretty much what one would expect of a Philadelphia lawyer in the nineteenth century.

An older cousin, William Rotch Wister, previously pursued a career in the law. "Rotch" was admitted to the bar in 1849, eleven years before Owen Wister was born. He lived on the Belfield Estate, the present site of La Salle University. He served as solicitor and director for many substantial financial institutions in Philadelphia, including the Philadelphia Contributionship and the National Bank of Germantown. Rotch was also an avid proponent of cricket and was a founding member of the Germantown Cricket Club. It seems only natural that Owen would want to follow in the footsteps of his older cousin, especially since Owen was attracted to and eventually married Rotch's daughter Mary Channing Wister. But Owen Wister followed another dream. He set out to be a musical composer. He studied music first at Harvard, where he graduated *summa cum laude*, and then for two years in Europe.

In 1885, Owen Wister returned to America and enrolled in Harvard Law School. While in law school, Wister was a frequent visitor at the residence of Oliver Wendell Holmes, who was then a justice of the Supreme Judicial Court of Massachusetts. In 1888, Wister graduated from Harvard Law School and returned to Philadelphia. Through his family connections he had the opportunity to serve an apprenticeship in the law office of Francis Rawle and Robert Ralston, at 402 Walnut Street.

Francis Rawle was a grandson of William Rawle, the first Chancellor of the Philadelphia Bar Association. Admitted to the bar in 1871, Francis Rawle was a "Legend of the Philadelphia Bar" in his own right. In 1878, he was one of the seventy-five lawyers who founded the American Bar Association at a meeting in Saratoga Springs, New York. Rawle was elected its first treasurer. In 1902, he was elected president of the ABA. He revised three editions of Bouvier's Law Dictionary. Francis was the Rawle who, in 1917, formed the partnership known as Rawle & Henderson. Francis Rawle was an ideal preceptor for an aspiring young lawyer with the educational and social background of Owen Wister.

Wister's work in the office of Rawle and Ralston was pretty much what one would expect of a new lawyer fresh out of law school. He assisted Ralston with the preparation of a new textbook. He represented a penniless widow in her efforts to acquire the assets of her recently deceased spouse. He handled small collection matters. He assisted Francis Rawle in bringing an unsuccessful trademark action, and then wrote the brief on appeal to the Supreme Court of Pennsylvania, *Putnam Nail Co. v. Dulaney,* 140 Pa. 205 (1891). It was basic stuff, the kind of work that has honed the skills of many young lawyers. But a young man whose close friends included the likes of Theodore Roosevelt and Oliver Wendell Holmes was not satisfied with such basic tasks.

Owen Wister found his work in the law office to be an "unpalatable grind." He complained that Rawle was "throwing him the crumbs." Wister sought the advice of Holmes, who had not particularly enjoyed the private practice of law. Holmes advised Wister to persevere with the law for a few more years before making a final decision. But Owen Wister had had enough. He sought a different career.

In 1892, *Harper's* retained Owen Wister, not to represent it, but to write short stories about the American West. Wister had been taking summer vacations hunting in Wyoming and other parts of the unsettled Rockies. He kept a journal of each trip. The journals provided the bases for his short stories. Wister pictured himself as an American Kipling, set on preserving in literature the culture of a short-lived American frontier. In 1902, Wister tied together several of his short stories and converted them into a cohesive novel.

The result was *The Virginian*. The book was dedicated to Wister's Harvard friend Theodore Roosevelt. Wister later wrote eleven other books, including a biography of Roosevelt, but none of them enjoyed the success of his landmark cowboy story.

People today are surprised to learn that Owen Wister was a lawyer. Six years of his life have been disregarded because of his spectacular success in another endeavor. Biographical summaries make only passing reference to Wister's legal career. For example, the *Encyclopedia Britannica* describes Wister as a "novelist" and devotes only one sentence to his lawyering.

The selective disregard of Wister's time as a lawyer is unfortunate. Owen Wister paid his dues to the legal profession. He attended and graduated from Harvard Law School. He served an apprenticeship of more than a year with a renowned Philadelphia lawyer, Francis Rawle. He was admitted to the bar in 1889, and practiced law for two years, including an appearance in the Supreme Court of Pennsylvania. Moreover, he continued to maintain a desk in Francis Rawle's law office at 328 Chestnut Street for another twenty years. Owen Wister is entitled to be called a Philadelphia lawyer. But when you call him that, *smile*.

JOHN G. JOHNSON:

The Giant of the Philadelphia Bar

©Philadelphia Bar Association, Reprinted with permission.

Giants are big. They stand head-and-shoulders above the rest of us and are physically dominant. Giants exist in many aspects of human endeavor; their accomplishments tower above those of their contemporaries. One thinks of Beethoven in music and Einstein in physics, each a giant in his own field.

In 1841, not even his own parents had any expectation that newborn John Graver Johnson would be a giant. His father, David Johnson, was a blacksmith. David died before his son finished high school. Elizabeth Johnson, who was a Graver and whose parents owned the farm at the end of the road that people called 'Graver's Lane,' took in sewing to support her small family. That was not the stuff of giants.

The house in which they lived was not a place where you would expect to find a giant. It was a diminutive woodframe building that still seems out of place at 8428 Germantown Avenue. The Johnsons were hardworking people without the advantages of wealth, college, law school or social status. Yet, their son exceeded all expectations. By the time of his death in 1917, John G. Johnson was hailed by The New York Times as "the greatest lawyer in the English-speaking world."

From the beginning, Johnson displayed strengths that were well-suited to a career in the law. He had a photographic memory. It was like having a personal computer a hundred years before computers were invented. He was decisive. He did not waste time agonizing over difficult decisions. He made the decision and his computerlike mind organized the supporting data instantaneously. He had a gift for advocacy that he developed into an art form. Instinctively, he knew what was persuasive to judges and juries. His arguments were not long-winded. He would select the most persuasive element of his position and then present a logical discussion of the facts of the case, returning time and time again to emphasize that one critical element. Observers said that it was like watching a man with a sledgehammer drive an iron spike into a railroad timber. Finally, Johnson was a workaholic. In his early years, hard work was necessary for survival — and Johnson's work became Johnson's life. He never turned down an assignment, be it as a scrivener, a messenger or a draftsman of legal documents. Gradually, he built up an expertise in both procedure and substantive law.

He argued one hundred sixty-eight cases in the Supreme Court of the United States and thousands of cases in the Supreme Court of Pennsylvania. Twice he was offered a seat on the Supreme Court of the United States; twice he declined the honor. George Wharton Pepper, in his autobiography, proclaimed Johnson to be "the most prodigious man I have ever known." He was a self-taught art collector whose Johnson Collection of nearly 1,300 paintings is the bulwark of the Philadelphia Museum of Art.

John Graver Johnson is the giant of the Philadelphia bar.

Johnson was admitted to the bar in February 1863, but his legal career was interrupted by a short stint in the military. In June that year, Johnson joined Battery A, First Pennsylvania Artillery, a unit that consisted almost entirely of members of the Philadelphia bar. As the Confederate Army advanced toward Gettysburg, Battery A was assigned to set up a defensive line west of Harrisburg. The Battle of Gettysburg lasted four days; it did not reach the battery at Harrisburg. Within thirty days, Johnson was back in his office practicing law.

Johnson was at home in his law office. Banker George W. Norris, in his book *Ended Episodes*, describes Johnson's office as follows: "[I]n the early Eighties, his office was an old dwelling house on the south side of Walnut Street, below Eighth. It consisted of a front and back parlor. In the front room were an assistant and one or two others. The wide double doors between the rooms were always open."

George Wharton Pepper, in *Philadelphia Lawyer, An Autobiography*, added this account: "Prominent lawyers from New York and other large cities were frequently to be seen in his anteroom, waiting their turn to enter his private office. Perhaps 'private' is the wrong word to use because his door was always open. Nobody was announced, people in waiting observed priorities among themselves as if they were approaching a box office; and as soon as one person came out, the man at the head of the line went in."

Johnson had little time for anything outside the office. He seems to have had no close friends. None of his contemporaries seemed to be his confidants. Rather, they talked about his idiosyncrasies, such as how he habitually lunched on a dozen oysters at a corner table — "his table" — of the Philadelphia Club, carefully placing a newspaper in front of him to discourage others from approaching.

Ironically, the law rescued Johnson's solitary social life. It was as though the law issued him both a wife and a ready-made family, ideally suited to a busy lawyer. One of his clients was an attractive young widow with three small children. Johnson was not able to reverse the business losses suffered by her late husband, but Johnson was successful in persuading Ida Powel Morrell to accept his proposal of marriage. Ida was a "one-L Powel" — a significant family in the society register of Old Philadelphia. Ida's standing opened to Johnson the doors of Old Philadelphia social clubs that otherwise would have excluded the blacksmith's son. Moreover, Ida was content to manage the children and the social aspects of the family, leaving her husband free to concentrate on the practice of law.

Johnson's early cases were primarily in the areas of property rights and decedent's estates, in effect an extension of his work before his admission to the bar. Given his familiarity with the law of property disputes, his photographic memory and his capacity for exhaustive work, Johnson was the logical choice to oversee the clearing of title for the transfer of League Island to the federal government for use as a Navy yard. He completed the task with apparent ease. That work persuaded the directors of the Pennsylvania Company to retain 28-year-old Johnson as its general counsel.

Almost immediately afterward, Johnson found himself in the Supreme Court of Pennsylvania in the company of five of Philadelphia's most respected lawyers, arguing an estate case dealing with the proposed Ridgway Library. Young Johnson exceeded the expectations of those lawyers. He argued that the law required the court to carry out the clearly stated instructions of the testator. His client prevailed; and the facade of the Ridgway Library still stands at Broad and Christian Streets as the frontispiece for the Philadelphia High School for the Performing and Creative Arts. It is a monument to Johnson's advocacy.

In 1884, Johnson argued his first case in the Supreme Court of the United States. More Supreme Court cases followed as Johnson's advocacy skills became known to businessmen in other geographic areas. Johnson's best-known local clients included Peter A.B. Widener and William L. Elkins, who made millions of dollars in the operation of horse-drawn and electrical streetcars. The Baldwin Locomotive Works was also a client, as was John Wanamaker. Now, J.P. Morgan, Henry Frick, Andrew Carnegie and Philip S. du Pont rushed to Johnson's door at the first sign of litigation. They expected Johnson to work magic with antitrust laws.

The American Sugar Refining Company controlled ninety-eight percent of the business of refining sugar at the time. The attorney general of the United States filed civil and criminal actions against the company and its officers alleging monopolization in violation of antitrust laws. Johnson represented the "Sugar Trust" — and he won the

case, convincing the court that the refining of sugar was not interstate commerce. Over the next dozen years, Johnson was sought out in antitrust cases to defend the American Tobacco Company, Northern Securities Company, Great Northern Railway, Northern Pacific Railway, Standard Oil Company and United States Steel Company. Historian Nathaniel Burt, in *The Perennial Philadelphians*, summed it up this way:
"What his friend J.P. Morgan was to finance, J.G. Johnson was to corporation law. The Trusts and Moguls of the Gilded Age 1900 wouldn't move without his advice, and Standard Oil and American Tobacco were merely two among his many similar clients. ... His opinions were considered equivalent among financiers to judicial decisions."

Like most of the lawyers of his day, Johnson was a sole practitioner. Still, he had able assistance because prestige was accorded to association with Johnson in the practice of law. Frank M. Prichard, an excellent lawyer in his own right, was associated with Johnson for thirty-four years. Prichard served as Chancellor of the Philadelphia Bar Association from 1915 through 1917. Another Johnson associate, Maurice B. Saul, founded a firm after Johnson's death that would later become Saul Ewing. Thomas D. Finletter became a highly respected judge of the Philadelphia Court of Common Pleas. Thomas Sovereign Gates became a vice president of Johnson's client Pennsylvania Company and later served as president of the University of Pennsylvania.

On the business side of the law, John G. Johnson paid little or no attention to the accumulation of wealth. Stories of his billings are legendary. George W. Norris, president of the Federal Reserve Bank of Philadelphia, noted in *Ended Episodes* that: "His charges were almost always extremely low, and for that reason he was not popular with other lawyers." Often, co-counsel would be embarrassed to learn that they had submitted bills that were substantially higher than those of the lead lawyer. Johnson is reputed to have submitted a bill to the Sugar Trust for the defense of its antitrust case in the total amount of just $3,000.

Judge Thomas D. Finletter, a former associate of Johnson, later told his judicial clerks of the time when Johnson was counsel on a securities offering, which entitled him to a fee of one penny for every share in the 1.5 million share offering. Johnson sent his client a bill for the total amount of $1,500. A few days later, the client came into Johnson's office, saying that there was a mistake in the billing. It should have been $15,000. He showed Johnson that the decimal point was misplaced. Johnson threw the fee bill back at the client and roared, "I am the lawyer. I decide what the bill shall be. You are the client; and your duty is to pay your bills!" Despite his disregard for high fees, the sheer volume of Johnson's law practice made him one of only three Philadelphia lawyers who earned more than $100,000 per year in the 1880s.

Judges recognized Johnson's genius and accorded him an unusually high level of respect. Contemporary lawyers modeled their legal documents on those drafted by Johnson and then defended the validity of the documents by citing Johnson as their source. Public figures sought Johnson's advice before making important decisions.

For example, George Wharton Pepper consulted Johnson after Pepper had been offered a position on the Circuit Court of Appeals. Johnson advised him to accept the offer; Pepper decided to decline. Most historians conclude that Johnson's advice was the wiser course of action. Clients from all walks of life flocked to Johnson's office and waited their turn to talk to the great lawyer. No matter how busy, Johnson always found the time to talk to everyone. Interestingly, George W. Norris observed in *Ended Episodes* that Johnson "was very profane, and did not modify his language to suit his client, but his profanity was so wholehearted and good-natured that it was never offensive."

By the early 1880s, Johnson developed an appreciation for art, particularly paintings. He approached the subject in a way one would expect of an accomplished trial lawyer: He studied the lives and works of great painters; he spoke to museum curators, art historians and dealers; and he visited art museums in America and in Europe.

In those days, the courts closed during the summer, when Johnson would book passage on a ship to Europe to visit art museums. To ward off the boredom of ten days at sea, Johnson took along as many mystery novels as he could carry. He would read one book after another, casting each volume overboard as soon as it was finished. Johnson's client Peter A.B. Widener, himself an accomplished art collector, sometimes accompanied Johnson on these trips and regularly engaged him in discussions about art.

In the fall of 1892, Johnson wrote a forty-four-page book titled *Sight-Seeing in Berlin and Holland Among Pictures*. It is a scholarly review and criticism of the Berlin Exhibition and other public and private collections in Berlin, Amsterdam, the Hague, Rotterdam and Scheveningnen. In this book, Johnson presented clear and authoritative analyses of painting after painting and artist after artist. Also, he evaluated the characteristics of the environment in which each painting was displayed. He was especially impressed with the illumination in the museum in Berlin, although not at all with the works exhibited there.

    Johnson brought to the world of art his meticulous research of chains of ownership, a database that proved invaluable in negotiating the purchase of works of art. Art curators, historians and dealers recognized Johnson's abilities and increasingly solicited Johnson's views on paintings. Johnson was convinced that a knowledgeable collector could assemble a significant collection of paintings by exercising good judgment and avoiding the purchase of paintings of lesser quality. Johnson set out to do just that. Again, he exceeded all expectations.

    Unlike most of the barons of American industry who hired art dealers to assemble their private collections, Johnson personally accumulated his collection. He had a keen eye for color, composition and artistic technique. He found that the very best paintings, the ones that would increase his enjoyment over a period of time, were often not the artist's best-known works. Johnson also was of the opinion that artists from different time periods displayed similar skills, and that the works of those artists were compatible with each other.

    He quickly ran out of wall space for his paintings. Paintings were crowded into every nook and cranny of his home at 426 South Broad Street. When he wanted to show a painting to a guest, Johnson would tell a member of his household staff where to find the painting and what it looked like. The staff person would then fetch the painting for inspection and afterward return it to its storage place.

As he neared 70, John Graver Johnson was reminded of his own mortality. In 1912, he took up the challenge of his last will and testament. He wanted to leave his art collection to the city of Philadelphia. However, he wanted the collection to be displayed in a setting that provided proper illumination, such a setting as existed in the Kaiser Friederich Museum in Berlin.

Philadelphia had no such art gallery. That was why Peter Widener left his valuable art collection to the National Gallery of Art in Washington, D.C. Johnson did not want to saddle Philadelphia taxpayers with the cost of constructing an expensive art gallery. Johnson was a member of the Fairmount Park Commission and he knew that the city had plans to build an art museum on Benjamin Franklin Parkway. He also knew from sad experience that such noble plans often fell by the wayside.

Meanwhile, Johnson may have been influenced by the decision of Henry Frick to construct a mansion that would, after his death, be home to the Frick Collection. Johnson was then living at 506 South Broad Street. In 1915, he purchased the adjoining residence at 510 South Broad Street and used it to exhibit his paintings.

It was not like Johnson to equivocate, but equivocate he did. He chopped and changed, writing codicils up until nearly the month before he died in April 1917.

Ultimately, Johnson left his art collection to the city of Philadelphia, conditioned upon the city agreeing to exhibit the collection at Johnson's residence at 510 South Broad Street. If the city did not accept the condition, the collection would go to the Metropolitan Museum of Art in New York.

Johnson's home on Broad Street bore no resemblance whatever to the Kaiser Friederich Museum. It also paled in comparison to Henry Frick's mansion. Any way you looked at it, it was a poor place to exhibit an exceedingly valuable art collection. In the final analysis, Johnson's equivocation assured that his will — like the testator — would spend much of its life in court.

In 1921, the city petitioned the orphans' court for permission to sell the real estate at 510 South Broad Street and to apply the proceeds toward the cost of the art museum that was to be built in Fairmount Park. A Master recommended approval, but Judge John Marshall Gest denied the petition on the well-established principle of law that the court should sustain the clearly stated intention of the testator to exhibit the paintings in his home on South Broad Street. The city would have to find another way to get the Johnson Collection out of the rundown building on South Broad Street.

In June 1933, five years after construction of the Philadelphia Museum of Art was completed, Johnson's paintings were moved there on a temporary basis. In the first year of its display at the museum, the Johnson Collection attracted almost 100,000 visitors, as compared with a single-year high of 11,388 during the years that it was exhibited in the South Broad Street residence.

In 1954, the trustee of Johnson's estate filed an account and petitioned the orphans' court for permission to exhibit the Johnson Collection at the museum on a permanent basis and also for permission to sell the real estate at 510 South Broad Street. President Judge Charles Klein reviewed the record and described the 1933 move of Johnson's artwork as "a clear violation of the city's contract with the executors … in open defiance of Judge Gest's order, an obvious disregard for the sanctity … of the solemn judgment of the orphans' court."

President Judge Klein was "not pleased." Eventually, Judge Klein did approve the exhibition of the Johnson Collection at the museum but required the trustees to report back to the court every ten years. In later years, further court decisions approved the integration of the Johnson Collection with non-collection works of art for exhibition purposes. In 1989, Judge Klein extended until December 31, 2083 the arrangement that will keep the Johnson Collection in the hands of the museum.

Philadelphia's Museum of Art is a place that commands one's attention. In location and design it dominates its surroundings. It is exactly the kind of place where you would expect to find a giant.

This is *OUR* Bar!

©Philadelphia Bar Association, reprinted with permission

"This is my bar."
Those were the words of Justice Bushrod Washington in the early 1800s as Philadelphia lawyers entered the U.S. Supreme Court. Judge Washington knew of whence he spoke. Nearly twenty years earlier, he "read the law" in Philadelphia under the direction of a preeminent Philadelphia lawyer, James Wilson. From the very beginning, Washington knew that Wilson was a lawyer of exceptional significance. That had to be the case. The study arrangements had been made personally by Washington's uncle, General George Washington.

In colonial Philadelphia, the preferred preparation for law was attendance at one of the Inns of Court in London. William Penn attended Lincoln's Inn. The other three Inns were Gray's Inn, Inner Temple and Middle Temple. The Inns of Court determined when an English lawyer was ready to be "called to the bar," i.e., admitted to practice. Between 1760 and 1783, more than 100 American lawyers received their training at the Inns of Court. That training was particularly valued in the middle colonies, and it left its mark on Philadelphia lawyers. One example is the Philadelphia tradition of listing the senior lawyer last and the junior lawyer first on court filings. That custom grew out of the practice at the Inns of Court, and it continued in Philadelphia until the latter half of the twentieth century.

With the War of Independence in 1776, Americans were no longer inclined to seek professional education in England. The way to become a lawyer in Philadelphia was "to read the law." In effect, it was an apprenticeship system. The "law clerk" or "law student" would work directly with a practicing lawyer who would also instruct his charges on the elements of the substantive law, which, for all practical purposes, were limited to equity, property and wrongs. The "tuition" varied from lawyer to lawyer, as did the quality of the preparation.

Even before the War of Independence, some Philadelphia lawyers were the products of the apprenticeship system. Andrew Hamilton emigrated from Scotland to the Chesapeake Peninsula of Virginia where he taught school while reading the law. He was admitted to the bar in 1703 and later undertook further studies at Gray's Inn pro favor. Apparently, pro favor meant that the skids were greased. Hamilton completed his studies in just two weeks. Nonetheless, the prestige of Gray's Inn may have played a part in Hamilton being retained to represent the family of William Penn, which representation brought him to Philadelphia in 1717. Hamilton served as recorder of Philadelphia, prothonotary of the Supreme Court and as a member of the Pennsylvania Assembly. It was in his capacity as an assemblyman in 1732 that he designed the building that we now call Independence Hall.

In 1735, the 59-year-old Hamilton took on the case that made him famous, the defense of printer John Peter Zenger who was accused of criminal libel against Bill Cosby. New York's Royalist Governor William Cosby had no sense of humor. The factual issue presented to the jury was whether Zenger had printed the offending material. Truth was not a defense to criminal libel. Hamilton argued that the jury should ignore the law as charged by the judge and instead return a general verdict of "not guilty." The verdict met with a mixed reaction. Legal scholars criticized it as contrary to law; patriots applauded the result. But everyone agreed that Zenger owed his freedom to the skill of his "smart Philadelphia lawyer." It took on a meaning of its own- "Philadelphia lawyer."

Thirty years after the Zenger case, another Scot came to America and became interested in the law. James Wilson taught at the College of Philadelphia, the school we now call the University of Pennsylvania. Seeing that lawyers in Philadelphia were generally affluent and well respected, Wilson borrowed money to read the law with Philadelphia lawyer John Dickinson, himself a product of three years at the Middle Temple. Wilson's law training was completed in less than a year. Finding that the supply of lawyers exceeded the demand for lawyering services in Philadelphia, he struck out in search of paying clients and courtroom experience. He traveled to the edge of the wilderness, which was then Carlisle, Pennsylvania. There, he developed an active courtroom practice riding a circuit that included Reading and Lancaster as well as Carlisle. Wilson signed both the Declaration of Independence and the Constitution. He was one of the most dynamic participants in the Constitutional Convention. On September 24, 1789, James Wilson was nominated by President George Washington to be an associate justice of the newly created U.S. Supreme Court. Wilson was not pleased. He wanted to be chief justice.

James Wilson

As the eighteenth century came to an end, Philadelphia was the center of government and the center of law in the United States. It was the largest city in the country, although its population would soon be eclipsed by the more densely populated New York. Philadelphia was the center of medicine. It was the center of science. It was the center of learning. Philadelphia was the center of insurance. It was also the center of finance and commerce, thanks largely to the

Bank of the United States. About 100 lawyers practiced full time in Philadelphia. For the most part, they were sole practitioners.

But times changed. The practice of law became more complex. The status of English common law in Pennsylvania courts was bitterly disputed. The importance of the growing federal, state and local case reports was apparent to everyone. But a well-prepared nineteenth-century lawyer still needed access to the traditional English law books. Faced with economic necessity, Philadelphia lawyers formed a professional association.

The Beginnings (1802-1852)

On March 13, 1802, The Law Library Company of the City of Philadelphia was created by a charter signed by seventy-one attorneys and approved by the three justices and the chief justice of the Pennsylvania Supreme Court. It was a stock company with shares at a par value of twenty dollars and annual dues of two dollars per member. The charter named as directors Joseph B. McKean, William Lewis, Edward Tilghman, William Rawle, Jasper Moylan, Joseph Hopkinson and John B. Wallace. The Law Library Company was located in the State House, i.e., Andrew Hamilton's "Independence Hall," in a small room adjoining the main building at the southeast corner. It stayed there until 1819 when it was moved to the second floor of Congress Hall, just west of the State House.

By and large, the lawyers of the early nineteenth century were a well-to-do lot. They were selected that way. In the first instance, not everyone in that era had the requisite education. Also, access to a practicing lawyer willing to sponsor the novice was a threshold barrier to entry into the legal profession. Horace Binney, 22 years of age when he signed the charter for the Law Library Company, would later recall that he waited eight years for his first opportunity to represent a major client in a major case. Young Binney's wait was made more tolerable by his appointment as the official reporter for the Pennsylvania Supreme Court. The official court reporter was an entrepreneur who kept the profits on all sales, just like any other bookseller. When success finally came, Binney quipped that Philadelphia lawyers owed much of their livelihood to the ingenuity of Napoleon Bonaparte. Bonaparte would not only confiscate the cargoes of ships taken on the high seas but would also justify the takings on novel grounds that did not fit neatly into the exclusions of commercial insurance policies. Rather than writing off the value of the ships and cargoes as would normally be done with acts of piracy or war, buyers, sellers and shipping companies brought suit against the insurers, usually in Philadelphia.

Horace Binney

The Law Library Company served its purpose reasonably well. In 1805, and again in 1811, William Rawle, an alumnus of London's Middle Temple, published catalogues of the books of the Law Library Company showing mainly English case reports and treatises on commercial law and maritime insurance. Rawle was an ideal person to maintain the records of the law library. His lawyer-grandfather had been admitted to the Philadelphia bar in 1725 and was a charter member of the Library Company of Philadelphia, which was founded by Benjamin Franklin in 1731.

In 1820, Philadelphia's lawyers addressed the need for training novice lawyers. The Law Academy of Philadelphia was patterned roughly after a short-lived lecture program presented by James Wilson in 1790. The first Provost was Peter S. DuPonceau who, as a teenager, left an abbey in

France and using his facility with languages, accompanied Baron Steuben to America. DuPonceau's linguistic ability led to his employment in a Philadelphia law office, and he was admitted to practice in 1785. President Thomas Jefferson offered DuPonceau an appointment as chief justice for Louisiana but he declined. He would rather be in Philadelphia.

In 1821, sixty-seven Philadelphia lawyers formed The Associated Members of the Bar of Philadelphia. It had two standing committees, a Committee of Censors and a Committee of Finance. Jared Ingersoll was elected Chancellor and Horace Binney was elected Vice Chancellor. The Associated Members of the Bar did not have a long life as a separate organization. On April 2, 1827, The Law Library Company merged with The Associated Members of the Bar to form The Law Association of Philadelphia. The corporate charter was the one issued to The Law Library Company in 1802. William Rawle was elected the first Chancellor and Horace Binney the first Vice Chancellor. More than 100 years later, the Association would change its name to the Philadelphia Bar Association.

The Second Bank of the United States on Chestnut Street near Fifth was a mainstay of Philadelphia's economy. When it opened in 1816, it had the full support of the secretary of the Treasury, Alexander J. Dallas. But by 1832, the bank had powerful enemies. One such enemy was President Andrew Jackson; another was "Old Hickory's" secretary of the Treasury, Philadelphia lawyer William J. Duane. Daniel Webster was the bank's main spokesman in the Senate. In the House, the leading advocate for the bank was Philadelphia lawyer Horace Binney, serving his only term in Congress. Webster and Binney succeeded in achieving legislation to renew the bank's charter, but Jackson vetoed the bill and instructed Duane to withdraw federal funds from the national bank. Duane refused. He opposed the national bank

Leave social security blank
Employer Name — Bell Telephone Co. of Penna.   Retired yes X

Gwendolyn Buhr, M.D., ~~TED~~ DURHAM

Emergency contact — Marcia 919-215-5380

~~919-419-4022~~
checks up ~~Tara~~ re
when ~~barber~~ is here

Right lower lobectomy
Low anterior resection w/ coloanal anastamosis
bladder diverticulectomy
Upper left wedge

but he would not destroy it. Jackson responded by removing Duane from office and replacing him with Attorney General Roger Brooke Taney (pronounced "Tawny") who carried out the President's order. The results were financial chaos and a severe depression. And Philadelphia was no longer the center of finance in the United States.

In the meanwhile, the Estate of Stephen Girard made its first appearance in Philadelphia's legal scene. Girard's heirs brought suit against the City of Philadelphia, seeking to set aside the multimillion-dollar bequest to establish the institution known as Girard College. A ruling that required a return of Girard's money would have been devastating. Fortunately, the Circuit Court ruled in favor of the city and dismissed the complaint. Girard's heirs appealed to the U.S. Supreme Court. Unexpectedly, the court listed the case for reargument. Girard's heirs sensed an opportunity for a reversal. Daniel Webster was retained to present their case at reargument. The city fathers, too, worried that the court had doubts, and now they were also worried about the fabled forensic skills of Webster. The city needed a new lawyer. The city needed Horace Binney. But Binney had retired from active practice. Hats in hand, the city fathers went to see Binney and pleaded with him to take one more case. Binney agreed to take on the representation but only on the condition that John Sergeant would stay on as co-counsel. Sergeant had read the law alongside Binney in the office of Jared Ingersoll.

Girard College

Binney found strong support for the validity of

Girard's bequest in the well-established law of England. His argument was unassailable. At the conclusion of the oral argument, Webster is reported to have said, "Mr. Binney, you buried my argument under a ton of granite." Not long after the Girard case was decided, Binney was offered, but declined, an appointment to the U.S. Supreme Court. Binney had the good sense to recognize that lawyering and adjudicating are two different skills. At heart, Binney was an advocate. His greatest skill was in gathering all of the available material relevant to an issue and then constructing the most persuasive argument possible in support of his asserted proposition. Twenty years later, he would again reject an appointment to the Supreme Court, this time upon the death of Chief Justice Roger B. Taney.

As the Law Association approached the end of its first half-century, its role as spokesman for the bar of Philadelphia expanded. Association leaders represented all Philadelphia lawyers in welcoming Chief Justice John Marshall on his many visits to the Philadelphia office of Dr. Philip Syng Physick. It was during these visits to the doctor that the Association commissioned the portrait of Chief Justice Marshall that still hangs today in its offices. In 1835, Chancellor William Rawle led the honor guard of lawyers that accompanied Marshall's body from Philadelphia back to Richmond, Virginia. And in 1850, virtually all of the leaders of the Law Association spoke out, albeit unsuccessfully, against a constitutional amendment that they believed would weaken the independence of the judiciary by making the judiciary an elected office. On the other hand, the election of judges marked the beginning of a

Chief Justice John Marshall

judiciary that more closely mirrored the make-up of Philadelphia's citizenry.

Philadelphia lawyers fretted about the qualifications of the young men entering the legal profession. In 1850, George Sharswood was appointed professor of law at the University of Pennsylvania. Sharswood was a well-respected judge of the Philadelphia Court. He would later be chief justice of the Pennsylvania Supreme Court and the author of a text upon which the rules of professional conduct would be based. Under Sharswood's direction, the university created an undergraduate law department and a two-year law program for part-time students. As a practical matter, the law department courses supplemented rather than replaced law office training. For most Philadelphians it was difficult to acquire even a high school education. Philadelphia had only one public high school, Central High School, which had just moved from the present site of the Wanamaker Building north to the corner of Broad and Green streets.

Lawyers' offices were in their homes, usually within walking distance of the courts located at Fifth and Chestnut streets. The parlor served as a reception area. Behind the parlor was a room occupied by a law clerk or law student with a desk or table and files. The lawyer had a small office in the back of the house. When no clients were in the office area, it was common for members of the family to use that space. The close proximity of the home offices of Philadelphia's lawyers brought those lawyers, their law clerks and their families into frequent social contact. Lawyers were, in effect, a family.

Philadelphia lawyers of this era also made their marks in distant locales. Richard Rush went to England as an agent of the United States and guided the will of James Smithson through the Court of Chancery. He returned to Washington with the bequest and helped to establish the Smithsonian

Institution. In the new state of Texas, a community on the Trinity River was named after Philadelphia lawyer George Mifflin Dallas who was then Vice President of the United States.

Workshop of The World
(1852-1902)

John Christian Bullitt was admitted to the bar in Kentucky. But Bullitt recognized the opportunity for lawyers in Philadelphia, where capital-intensive industries were taking root and business corporations were creating new law. Before long, Bullitt was joined in practice by a former librarian of the Law Library Company, Samuel Dickson. Corporations needed counsel with respect to organization and reorganization. The practice of law was moving out of the courtrooms and into lawyers' offices.

Philadelphia's industrial capability became even greater during the Civil War. Philadelphia was the northern city closest to the Confederacy. It was a natural manufacturing and supply point for the Union's war effort. But in Philadelphia's business community there was substantial sympathy for the Confederate cause, and that sympathy was shared by many lawyers. Bluntly stated, it was good business. Robert D. Coxe, an active member of the Law Association, in a retrospective tribute praised lawyers Edward Hopper, George H. Earle, Sr., William S. Pierce and Charles Gibbons for their anti-slavery leadership, and noted that: "The championship of so desperate and so unpopular a cause demanded physical, no less than moral courage on the part of its advocates. The bar, as a body, conservatively gave it the cold shoulder, and Mr. Hopper and his associates were, in truth, the victims, frequently, of positively uncivil treatment at the hands of their brother lawyers."

Lawyers in the antebellum era left something to be desired when dealing with a moral issue that had adverse economic consequences.

When the Confederate army moved north into south central Pennsylvania in 1863, the reality of war hit home. The Confederates were spoiling for a fight. There was a genuine fear that General Lee's battle-hardened army would veer to the east and make an all-out attack on Philadelphia, less than 100 miles distant. The lead element of Confederate General Ewell's army was just a few miles west of Harrisburg, approaching the Susquehanna River. Defending the state capital was none other than a contingent of Philadelphia lawyers.

A reserve unit created at the urging of Horace Binney in 1844 (to help maintain the peace after violent anti-Catholic riots) had been reactivated in 1861 as Battery A, First Pennsylvania Artillery. It was staffed by volunteers from the Philadelphia bar, among them George Washington Biddle, William Henry Rawle, Charles E. Morgan (who would later form a partnership with Francis D. Lewis and later still be joined by Morris Bockius), Clement B. Penrose, C. Stuart Patterson, Charles Chauncey, Henry D. Landis, and James T. Mitchell, who would become chief justice of the Pennsylvania Supreme Court. But the most interesting of all was a tall, slender 21-year-old who seemed out of place in such elegant company, Private John Graver Johnson.

Pvt. John G. Johnson

People like Johnson were not supposed to be lawyers. His father had been a blacksmith. His widowed mother took in sewing to make ends meet. Johnson worked day and night to help support his mother and two younger brothers. In his last year of high school, Johnson was offered a job by lawyer Benjamin Rush, a grandson of the colonial doctor. What Rush had in mind was employment as a messenger, not as a law student. By sheer persistence of will, Johnson worked himself up to law student status. When Benjamin Rush retired, Johnson went to work for Rush's brother, J. Murray Rush and, upon Murray's death, Johnson went to the office of another Rush kin, Henry J. Williams. Johnson's weighty domestic responsibilities seemed to explain why he labored day and night on an ever-increasing number of real estate leases and small decedent's estates. It helped that Johnson was a quick reader. He also had a photographic memory.

Williams' most important client was the Pennsylvania Company, which, in 1842, had foreclosed on and taken possession of a small (one league in circumference) island in the Delaware River at the southern tip of Philadelphia. For more than a quarter of a century, the Pennsylvania Company tried to unload its unwanted island. Then someone came up with the idea that Philadelphia should give League Island to the federal government for use as a modern naval base. It was an offer that the federal government could not refuse. The Pennsylvania Company looked to its lawyers to oversee the transaction quickly through to closing. Johnson handled all aspects of the transaction with apparent ease.

Not long after the Navy Base transaction, Dr. James Rush died. His will named his brother-in-law, Henry J. Williams, as his executor and awarded the residue of his estate to the Library Company of Philadelphia for the express purpose of building a library as a memorial to his late wife, Phoebe Ann Ridgway. Philadelphia newspapers were ecstatic at the prospect of a million-dollar gift for public use. The Library Company was ecstatic at the prospect of a magnificent new building. But then Henry Williams disclosed that on his deathbed, James Rush insisted that the library be built on the property at Broad and Christian streets, a full nine blocks south of Center Square. The Board of the Library Company had in mind a location closer to the hub of the city.

The Library Company Board included the most prestigious judges and lawyers in Philadelphia. The Board accepted the bequest and then filed a Bill in Equity to enjoin the construction of the library at Broad and Christian streets. The court granted an injunction, and Williams appealed to the Pennsylvania Supreme Court. Attorneys for Williams were former Chief Justice George W. Woodward, George Junkin and John G. Johnson. Representing the Library Company were William Henry Rawle, the brilliant but acidic Richard McMurtrie, and former Secretary of the Treasury William M. Meredith. The argument extended over the course of three days. Williams was portrayed as a present-day Don Quixote, pursuing a quest that no one else could understand. In marked contrast to the emotional presentations of the senior advocates was the calm, steady, high-pitched voice of the much-younger John G. Johnson, whose great height and slender build gave him a unique courtroom presence.

Johnson's argument made sense. Absent fraud or incapacity, the court should not interfere with the discretionary authority of an executor. Johnson repeatedly hammered home the undeniable good faith of Williams and the equally undeniable fact that he was acting in the express interest of the testator. The Supreme Court reversed the decree and removed the restraint on Williams. Ninety years after its construction, the Ridgway Library was sold to the City of Philadelphia. Its imposing facade of Doric columns now serves as the frontispiece on Broad Street for the Philadelphia High School for the Creative and Performing Arts, a remnant of nineteenth-century fancy preserved by twentieth-century respect for the past. Precious few passersby recognize it as a memorial to the advocacy of John G. Johnson.

The Chestnut Hill blacksmith's son was the most sought after lawyer in Philadelphia. There were now about 1,000 lawyers in Philadelphia, only 400 of them members of the Law Association. When lawyers died, their clients tended to migrate to the offices of friends or relatives of the deceased. In a world of sole practitioners and two- and three-lawyer partnerships, a long life span almost assured the success of a competent lawyer who had the proper family connections. Only about 100 Philadelphia lawyers earned more than $5,000 per year. At the top were a handful that included John C. Bullitt, his partner Samuel Dickson, and John G. Johnson, each of whom was reportedly earning more than $100,000 annually. Charles E. Morgan and George W. Biddle were not doing badly either.

In the meanwhile, the locus of the legal community was moving west from Independence Hall. In December 1872, the Law Association moved its offices to a third-floor location on Walnut Street, west of Sixth Street. Four years later, it moved one block south to the Athenaeum Building on South Sixth Street. The city's prime residential area had already moved west of Broad Street to the neighborhood surrounding Rittenhouse Square.

The Constitution of 1873 created four courts of general jurisdiction, Common Pleas Courts Numbers 1, 2, 3 and 4, each having three judges, one of whom was the president judge. This system of numbered 3-judge courts would last for ninety-five years, and the separate courts reached a total of ten. Philadelphia's courts were crammed into whatever space was available in and around Independence Hall. The courtrooms were in deplorable condition. George W. Norris, who covered Philadelphia courts for the newspapers while studying for admission to the bar, observed: "It would tax the imagination of the practitioners of today [1937] to imagine how bare and dingy these rooms were. There were no draperies, no marble or hardwood ornamentations . . . Most of the rooms were heated by stoves, and gas was the only illuminant." It was in the late 1880s that it became customary for the judges to wear black robes on the bench, a symbol of decorum and respect. Typical court practice involved a five-and-one-half day week. Trials were conducted on Monday through Friday, and motion lists were heard on Saturday mornings. On the other hand, courts closed after the May term and did not reopen until September. Successful lawyers in those days had real summer vacations.

It was becoming painfully evident that the emerging corporations could wreak harm as well as confer benefit. Congress took steps to regulate abusive practices in public service industries. The government guaranteed monopoly power but imposed strict governmental regulation on those businesses. Public service regulation began with the railroads. In 1887, the Interstate Commerce Act was passed. New concepts emerged in regulatory law. "Operating rights," i.e., formal authority to participate in a regulated business, became not only a concept of law but also a valuable commodity that could be bought and sold. Regulation of rates gave rise to juridical economics and concepts of "fair rate of return" on the "fair value" of assets "used and useful" in the public service. Hard economic reality was blended with hypothesis and legal theory. And, of course, public utility regulation expanded the work of lawyers.

New laws were also enacted to apply juridical economics to private enterprise. On July 2, 1890, Congress enacted the Sherman Antitrust Act to protect trade and commerce from the predatory practices of monopolies. It was not long before the Justice Department saw an opportunity to flex its Sherman Act muscle. In March 1892, four Philadelphia sugar refiners merged into the American Sugar Refining Company. The merger gave the resulting company complete control of the manufacture of sugar in the United States. The attorney general brought suit to enjoin the combination of sugar manufacturers popularly known as "The Sugar Trust." Defending the case was Philadelphia lawyer John G. Johnson. No longer slender and now sporting a bushy mustache, Johnson followed his classic courtroom approach, selected a major point and drove it home with clear, forceful argument. Johnson convinced the court that manufacturing is different from commerce, and that only monopolization of commerce is proscribed by the antitrust laws.

John G. Johnson

Johnson represented a large number of clients. Still, he remained available to the average person. Lawyers shook their heads in disbelief when Johnson refused to travel to New York City to consult with J.P. Morgan. He was too busy to leave his office. So Morgan came to Johnson's office in Philadelphia-and waited his turn while Johnson met with the everyday clients who were first in line. Johnson represented the tobacco industry, Northern Pacific Railroad, U.S. Steel and Standard Oil Company. Johnson also represented Peter A.B. Widener and George Elkins in obtaining the right to operate electric trolleys in Philadelphia. The bar's admiration for Johnson was offset by its consternation over his billing practices. In those days no one kept time records. Fee bills were submitted at the end of the case. Johnson is reputed to have billed the Sugar Trust only $3,000 for the defense of its antitrust case. Co-counsel were often embarrassed to learn that they had billed amounts significantly higher than the lead counsel had.

In 1898, the courts, the Law Association and the Law Library completed their move into Philadelphia's present City

Hall. The South Portal of City Hall is dedicated to the theme of justice. It includes a sculpture of the face of Horace Binney, one of only three sculptures of real people on the exterior of the massive building. The other two people so depicted are William Penn and Benjamin Franklin.

Lawyers' office buildings changed, too. With the development of fireproofing for steel girders and with the availability of electric-powered elevators, tall buildings sprouted up near the new City Hall. In 1897, the sixteen-story Land Title Building at Broad and Chestnut streets was built as a speculative office building. Five years later, a taller second tower was added. Lawyers flocked to offices in the new skyscrapers, particularly the Land Title Building. The days of the home law office were over. Law offices now were strictly places to work. Philadelphia's most desirable residential area was no longer Rittenhouse Square. In fact, it was no longer in Philadelphia. Affluence followed the main line of the Pennsylvania Railroad to the spacious areas with old-world names, Bryn Mawr, Berwyn, Strafford and Devon.

Advances in technology also changed the face of Philadelphia's law offices. The typewriter made professional scriveners obsolete almost overnight. Appellate briefs were usually printed, an expensive, time-consuming process that was virtually monopolized in Philadelphia by Allen, Lane & Scott. And then there was the telephone. The telephone was relatively slow in gaining acceptance by lawyers. It is easy to understand why lawyers would be resistant to using a contraption that required the speaker to shout into a mouthpiece, thereby sharing the conversation with anyone within earshot.
As the Law Association of Philadelphia reached its 100th year, it showed signs of age.

Nothing was in obvious disrepair but there was a trace of mild decay, a suspicion that the venerable institution might be ill suited to the gathering demands of the twentieth century. An estimated 1,500 lawyers practiced in Philadelphia, less than half of them were members of the Association. The Bar Association of the twentieth century would evolve from the interaction of the traditional practice of law with intensive academic thought, legislative process, law-making power, industrial change, technological advances and continuing social progress, all wrapped in two world wars and tempered by a Great Depression. The Bar Association that emerged from that unrelenting process would scarcely have been recognized by Jared Ingersoll or any of the other charter members of the Law Library Company.

Turbulent Times
(1902-1952)

In many respects, the turn-of-the-century Bar Association was its own worst enemy. The Association was largely the product of Philadelphia's privileged class. The Old Philadelphia character of the bar began to change as full-time law schools assumed the primary role in the preparation of new lawyers. Full-time law schools also enabled scholars to devote themselves to the principles underlying the law in an industrial society in which courts of the separate states act independent of each other.

William Draper Lewis, the energetic dean of the University of Pennsylvania Law School, insisted that law professors devote full time to teaching and improving the law. He eliminated from the faculty the practicing lawyers and judges. In 1914, Lewis ran for governor of Pennsylvania. He lost, but his campaign proposals for a Child Labor Law and a Workmen's Compensation Law were enacted by the Legislature the following year.

Lewis was also active in the Association of American Law Schools. He was secretary of the Committee on the

Establishment of a Permanent Organization for the Improvement of the Law. That committee recommended an American Law Institute to provide guidance to lawyers and judges throughout the land. It was created in 1923. William Draper Lewis was its founding director, which resulted in ALI being located in Philadelphia.

Philadelphia and its lawyers were also affected by changes emanating from Washington. In 1913, the Sixteenth Amendment to the Constitution empowered Congress "to lay and collect taxes on incomes," thereby creating a new species known as the tax lawyer. In 1914, Congress continued its efforts to regulate the economy with the adoption of the Federal Reserve Act. The Federal Highways Acts, beginning in 1916, gave a great boost to lawyers who specialized in personal injury actions. The establishment of a nationwide network of highways, however, eventually brought to an end Philadelphia's predominant manufacturing power. The highways freed manufacturers from their dependence on railroads and enabled businesses to relocate in other geographic areas. The decline was imperceptible at first. It would take nearly fifty years for the full effect to be felt. But eventually, manufacturing plants would be abandoned, lingering environmental hazards would be discovered, and Philadelphia neighborhoods would be left without their traditional source of economic support.

Closer at hand, the career of Philadelphia's greatest trial lawyer moved inexorably toward the end. On April 16, 1917, John Graver Johnson died. The United States Steel case was on appeal to the Supreme Court. Johnson's death was reported in newspapers across the country. The New York Times stated that he was "in the opinion of some well-qualified judges, the greatest lawyer in the English-speaking world." Johnson's magnificent art collection of about 1,300 paintings (he was a self-taught authority) was left to the City of Philadelphia. It is the premier collection of the Philadelphia Museum of Art.

John G. Johnson's courtroom record remains for posterity. Johnson is credited by his biographer with handling an incredible 168 arguments in the U.S. Supreme Court (few lawyers today have handled as many as ten). Also, he handled about 2,000 cases in the Pennsylvania Supreme Court, 198 cases in the U.S. Circuit Court of Appeals, 83 cases in the Pennsylvania Superior Court, and more than 200 cases in other courts, while maintaining a substantial corporate and securities law practice. Like most lawyers of his day, Johnson was a sole practitioner. His law practice was appropriated by his associates who then formed the firm of Prichard, Saul, Bayard & Evans. In 1923, that firm split into Evans, Bayard & Frick, and Saul, Ewing, Remick & Saul.

Sole practice was giving way to the big law firms. John C. Bullitt recognized the need for continuing legal advice, but it was his partner, Samuel Dickson, who brought in Henry S. Drinker and continued the metamorphosis of Bullitt's practice to today's Drinker Biddle & Reath. Morgan, Lewis & Bockius has had the same firm name since Morris Rex Bockius became a "name" partner in 1908. Duane, Morris & Heckscher began as a firm in 1904. Lawyers named "Rawle" have practiced in Philadelphia since the early 1700s but Rawle & Henderson began in about 1917. Messrs. Ballard, Spahr, Andrews & Ingersoll were all in the same firm by 1920. George Wharton Pepper's two-lawyer partnership slowly became Pepper Hamilton. Roberts, Montgomery, and McKeehan continues today as Montgomery, McCracken, Walker & Rhoads. And a background in genealogy is helpful to anyone trying to trace the ancestors of Dechert, Price & Rhoads. In the 1920s, these were the Old Philadelphia law firms. Typically, the "big firms" of the 1920s ranged in size from four to six partners. And typically, each of those firms had at least one outstanding courtroom lawyer.

George Wharton Pepper was one of the best-known Philadelphia lawyers. Pepper had a prodigious memory. He never spoke from notes. And he loved to quote at length from Gilbert & Sullivan. In 1922, Pepper was appointed to the U.S. Senate upon the death of Boies Penrose. Pepper then won a general election to fill Penrose's unexpired term. "Senator George Wharton Pepper," it had a prestigious ring. Pepper enjoyed being at the source of power and he also enjoyed the opportunities to display his broad range of interests and his knowledge of competent individuals, as he did in the matter involving Salt Creek.

Salt Creek, Wyoming, was the site of one of three federal petroleum reserves. Very few people recognize the name Salt Creek. It is more commonly known by reference to a local geological formation as "Teapot Dome." The federal oil reserves were valued in excess of $100,000,000 and questions were being raised about the reserves having been leased to private interests without public disclosure and without competitive bidding. The Senate needed an independent special counsel to conduct an investigation; but who would have the confidence of the nation? Senator George Wharton Pepper suggested a Philadelphia lawyer.

Owen Josephus Roberts was the son of a Germantown hardware merchant, and he had been a law student when Pepper taught at the University of Pennsylvania. Teapot Dome was the major political scandal of the 1920s. The attention of the nation was riveted on the investigation and the prosecution. Owen J. Roberts emerged as a

Owen J. Roberts

national hero. In 1930, President Herbert Hoover nominated Roberts as an associate justice of the U.S. Supreme Court. His approval by Congress was a foregone conclusion.

Philadelphia lawyer William A. Schnader, a protégée of William Draper Lewis, in 1922 became a special deputy to the attorney general of Pennsylvania for the express purpose of drafting the legislation necessary to carry out the reorganization of the state government. Between 1923 and 1935, the Pennsylvania Legislature adopted a new Administrative Code, a Fiscal Code, a new Business Corporation Law, a new Non-Profit Law, a new Banking Code, a new Department of Banking Code, a Building and Loan Association Code and an Insurance Code. After returning to private practice in 1935, Schnader took the lead of the Commissioners on Uniform State Laws and, working with the American Law Institute, led the effort that resulted in the nationwide adoption of the Uniform Commercial Code.

Schnader was joined in private practice by Deputy Attorney General Bernard G. Segal. At their first meeting in Harrisburg, Segal made it a point to tell Schnader that he, Segal, was a Jew, explaining that "in eminent Philadelphia law firms there are no Jews, and . . . the firm with which you were connected is one of them." Segal's concern was not new.

Mayer Sulzberger felt that way forty years earlier. Sulzberger was born in Baden, Germany, in 1843. His father was a teacher; his grandfather a rabbi. His parents came to Philadelphia in 1848. Mayer Sulzberger attended high school and later worked in the law office of Moses Aaron Dropsie. He was admitted to the bar in 1865. An intelligent and thorough lawyer, he was a rising star in the Philadelphia courts and was prominent in the American Jewish community. Unexpectedly, in 1894, Sulzberger cut short his career as a lawyer. He accepted a position as a judge in the

Court of Common Pleas No. 2. George W. Norris was of the view that Sulzberger took the judicial office in the hope that the prestige of the position would reflect favorably on other Jewish lawyers and make easier the career paths of future generations. When he retired from the bench in 1916, there were still no Jews in the firms of Old Philadelphia lawyers. Sulzberger may well have wondered if his sacrifice had been worth the effort.

Sulzberger need not have wondered. Horace Stern knew and admired Sulzberger. Stern was one of eight children in a North Philadelphia family that struggled mightily to make ends meet. He won a scholarship to the University of Pennsylvania, graduating in 1899; and then won the one scholarship offered by the university's law school. After graduating summa cum laude, Stern stayed on at the law school as a lecturer. In the fall of 1903, he formed a law partnership with Morris Wolf. By the 1930s, their firm, then called Wolf, Block, Schorr & Solis-Cohen, was the Jewish law firm in Philadelphia. But Horace Stern had chosen a different path. In 1920, Stern accepted an appointment as judge of the Court of Common Pleas No. 2, which many Philadelphia lawyers referred to as the "Jewish Court." It had been Mayer Sulzberger's court. However, Stern was not content to stay in C.P. No. 2. In 1935, Horace Stern was elected to the Pennsylvania Supreme Court; and in 1952 he became chief justice, taking the quest of Mayer Sulzberger to new heights.

Lawyers without social or economic ties to existing business often turned their attention to the growing field of personal injury practice. With the rapid growth of public utilities, the expansion of public transportation and the widespread use of motor vehicles, the number of negligence claims was skyrocketing. Entrepreneurial lawyers set out to capture this growing segment of business in a fashion that offended traditional lawyers. For example, they used representation agreements in which fees were stated as a percentage of the recovery and were contingent upon there being a recovery.

In March 1928, the Law Association instituted an investigation of "the practice of the solicitation of contingent fee accident cases," a subject often referred to as "ambulance chasing." The investigating committee was prestigious. Henry S. Drinker Jr. was the chairman. Members included Franklin E. Barr, Frederic L. Ballard, John Arthur Brown, Francis A. Lewis III, Benjamin H. Ludlow, William Clarke Mason, Lemuel B. Schofield and Richardson Dilworth, who served as assistant to the chairman. The committee found that "a contingent fee agreement is necessary for the protection of the general run of injured persons." Taken as a whole, the report was straightforward and well reasoned. However, it has played an unfortunate role in the history of the Bar Association.

Social historians view the "ambulance chasing" investigation together with the subject of standards proposed for admission to the bar as part of a well-orchestrated effort to prevent immigrants from practicing law. Invariably, this view is supported by quotes, such as that attributed to Henry S. Drinker that purports to explain that the solicitation network was the result of lawyers "who, having come 'up out of the gutter . . . were merely following the methods their fathers had been using selling shoe-strings and other merchandise.'" The same historians also quote Robert McCracken as crediting preceptorship rules with reducing the number of immigrants who applied for admission to the bar in Pennsylvania. The "ambulance chasing" investigation also gave the appearance of being a vendetta carried out by the Association at the behest of the Old Philadelphia firms against less-affluent Philadelphia lawyers; the acrimonious relationship of these two groups within the Association would persist for more than fifty years. Legal Philadelphia was an adversarial place, and those who shared a common enemy tended to band together.

One such band was the "Caveat Club." It began with a small group of Irish Catholic lawyers who regularly challenged each other's statements. It was the proponent's obligation to prove the accuracy of the disputed matter. After losing a few challenges-and enduring the jibes that went with the losses-speakers were advised to "beware" or "caveat," lest the experience be repeated. Thus, the name "Caveat Club" came into being. From that humble beginning, the group expanded its membership beyond Irish Catholics. The Caveat Club brought a new weapon to bear upon the established leadership of the Bar Association: humor. It was a quality that Peter F. Hagan, James P. Crumlish, Joseph S. Lord III, John P. Boland, Nochem Winnet, Charles Klein and many other Philadelphia lawyers had in abundance. Eventually the energy of the club was focused on the Bar Association elections, and the Old Philadelphia hold on the office of Chancellor was broken. The Caveat Club's unofficial "chairman," Walter B. Gibbons, served as Chancellor in 1943 and 1944, the first non-establishment Chancellor of the Philadelphia Bar Association.

While the lawyers of the Caveat Club struggled to achieve parity with Philadelphia's big-firm lawyers, African Americans struggled just to get a foot in the door. Blacks have been a part of Philadelphia since the time of William Penn. Their experience has been varied. It includes elite families who, in many respects, were a mirror image of "Old Philadelphia" society. They valued education, music and art. The Pyramid Club regularly presented art and cultural events featuring the work of black artists and performers. The Philadelphia Cotillion Society annually sponsored formal, invitation-only cotillions that rivaled the Assemblies of "Old Philadelphia." Like other Philadelphia groups, African Americans were adversely affected by an influx of lesser-educated "newcomers." But there were also major differences between the African-American experience and the experience of immigrant groups. Eighteenth and nineteenth century African Americans did not have economic or social clout. None of Philadelphia's blacks owned a dominant business or commanded widespread public allegiance so as to be able to marshal the resources of the black community, much less the community as a whole.

And then there was the specter of racism that has always been present in American society. Philadelphia as a whole did not support slavery, and Pennsylvania was among the first states to abolish slavery altogether. Nonetheless, the rules of everyday life were tipped decidedly against blacks, especially in employment, housing and the enforcement of penal laws. It was not an environment conducive to the development of black lawyers. Students of the subject differ as to when the first black Philadelphia lawyer appeared on the scene. Geraldine R. Segal, in her study of the black legal community, cites Henry Johnson and Isaac Parvis, who were identified as "lawyers" in the Census of 1850. Over the next fifty years, only thirteen black lawyers appear to have practiced in Philadelphia. Only a few of those lawyers could afford to devote full time to the practice of law in a system in which the outcome of disputes depended exclusively on determinations made by white judges and white juries. Even black businessmen tended to retain white lawyers.

In 1888, Aaron Mossell became the first black to graduate from the Law Department of the University of

Pennsylvania. In 1921, Mossell's academic achievement was eclipsed by his daughter Sadie, who became the first black woman to receive a Ph.D. from the University of Pennsylvania. In 1923, Sadie Tanner Mossell married Harvard law student Raymond Pace Alexander, a member of one of the "Old Philadelphia" black families. Not to be outdone by her husband, Sadie Alexander then obtained a law degree from the University of Pennsylvania, the first black woman to do so, and joined her husband in private practice. Their office was located on South 19th Street; major Philadelphia office buildings did not lease space to blacks.

Raymond Pace Alexander

The years between 1910 and 1930 saw the first major surge of black migration into the city. Most of those migrants were sharecroppers and agricultural laborers who toiled in the fields, often for a subsistence living. In 1890, Philadelphia had a population of 39,371 blacks. By 1930, the number of blacks had increased to 219,599. They came to Philadelphia pursuing a dream of industrial employment. The dream was an illusion. They arrived unwelcome, unemployed and ill prepared for the hostile urban environment that awaited them.

That hostile environment was almost enough to make J. Austin Norris give up the practice of law. Norris, who was born in Chambersburg, Pennsylvania, graduated from Yale Law School in 1917. After a two-year stint in the segregated U.S. Army, Norris settled in Philadelphia and began a criminal defense law practice. Norris quickly recognized the plight of black lawyers. More important, he formulated a response to that plight; he would develop political power.

"Power respects power" was the way that one of his partners described the outlook of Austin Norris. In 1932, Norris became the political leader of the Seventh Ward, which ran from Spruce Street to South Street and from Seventh Street to the Schuylkill River. In 1937, he was appointed to Philadelphia's Board of Revision of Taxes. At about the same time, a handful of blacks, including Harvey N. Schmidt, Thomas Reed and Eugene Clarke, were working at the post office by day and attending Temple Law School at night, anticipating the opportunity to enter the practice of law.

The challenges that confronted women who wanted to practice law bore similarities to those facing African Americans. Women were excluded from the practice of law by a deep-seated cultural bias that was built into the established rules and that would be overcome only with great effort, beginning in the 1880s and extending into the latter part of the twentieth century. Caroline Burnham Kilgore had to fight for the opportunity just to sit in on the lectures at the law department of the University of Pennsylvania. She first applied in 1870 and was refused. She read the law in her husband's law office, sought admission through the Board of Examiners in 1874 and was refused on the ground that women were not eligible to practice in the courts of Pennsylvania. After unsuccessfully pressing the Legislature for a remedy, she reapplied to the university in 1881, and the request was granted. Upon completion of the two-year course, Kilgore applied to each of the Philadelphia Courts and was admitted only to the Orphans' Court and C.P. No. 4 on the order of Judge Thayer. Her applications were also viewed favorably by Common Pleas Judges William S. Pierce and Thomas K. Finletter, albeit in dissenting opinions. Full admission to the bar finally came in 1886, after the Legislature amended the prior law.

For a while, it appeared as though Carrie Kilgore's efforts on behalf of women had gone for naught. Few women entered law schools, and the ones that did obtain a legal education sought employment outside the law. But gradually, other women entered the profession. In many cases, those women were wives of practicing lawyers, and they appear to have had little interest in their own practice. Bar Association publications often referred to them as "Portias," a term that many women lawyers consider demeaning. It was difficult for women lawyers to survive in an environment where they were not accepted as equals by commercial clients, by other members of the bar and by the judiciary. As a result, women lawyers often looked to government employment and to the practice of domestic relations law.

Sadie Alexander took a part-time position as an assistant city solicitor. In 1932, Hazel Hemphill Brown gravitated naturally to the Domestic Relations Division of the District Attorney's Office. Not only did Brown have an academic and occupational background in social work, but she also was at home in the Municipal Court. In 1914, her father, Judge Charles L. Brown, helped establish the Municipal Court and became its president judge. Hazel Brown also maintained a private practice in the office of Caroline K. Kenworthy. Lois G. Forer graduated from Northwestern University Law School in 1938. She came to Philadelphia and found employment as a clerk for Judge John C. Biggs in the Third Circuit Court of Appeals.

The bar was changing. New laws, new administrative agencies and new rules of procedure were increasing the demand for lawyers. But the supply did not keep pace with the increasing demand. It was a matter of hard economic fact. The Great Depression put the legal profession out of reach for most of the population. Few jobs were available. Savings were depleted or lost entirely. The cost of college and law school education was prohibitive. Until the Depression passed, the supply of lawyers in Philadelphia would not increase significantly, regardless of what happened on the demand side of the equation.

The cure was worse than the Depression. President Franklin Delano Roosevelt sounded the alarm in a dramatic address that has become a significant part of American history: "Yesterday, December 7, 1941-a date which will live in infamy-the United States of America was suddenly and deliberately attacked by naval and air forces of the Empire of Japan." The attack was devastating. Pearl Harbor, the principal naval base in the Pacific, lay smoldering, along with eighteen war ships sunk or badly damaged, more than 200 aircraft destroyed or damaged, and more than 3,500 Americans dead, missing or wounded. The country wanted to know why it had happened. To answer that question, Roosevelt turned to a Philadelphia lawyer, Owen J. Roberts, then an associate justice of the Supreme Court.

Compared with the extensive Teapot Dome investigation and prosecution, the work of the Roberts Commission was very brief. But the subject matter was of extreme importance, and the proceeding took place under circumstances of emergency wartime mobilization. The Commission found that the commanders of the Army and Navy were derelict in failing to consult and confer with each other to assure the defense of Pearl Harbor. It did not delve into the complex and sophisticated questions of changing military technology or the need for new diplomatic and military attitudes and procedures. That was left for a later day. Once again, Owen Roberts answered the call of his country. After hostilities ceased, two other Philadelphia lawyers were called upon by the President for exceptional service: Francis Biddle to serve as a judge on the Nuremberg War Crimes Court; and Earl G. Harrison to report on the treatment of Jews who had survived their internment in Nazi concentration camps.

A lingering image from the Second World War is that of six U.S. Marines in February 1945, reaching upward, straining to unfurl the Stars and Stripes into a stiff wind atop Mount Suribachi on the small volcanic island called Iwo Jima. Three decades later, Philadelphia lawyer James J. McEldrew Jr. would reluctantly recall Mount Suribachi, but his memory was not of a flag, but rather a large iron drainage pipe that ran down the slope to the Pacific Ocean. McEldrew thanked God for that iron pipe. A 19-year-old Marine rifleman, just two years removed from Philadelphia's West Catholic High School, McEldrew pressed his back hard against that drainpipe. It was his only protection from the blizzard of bullets and artillery shells bursting around him. Then, he leaned forward, grasped his broken leg, and slid inch-by-inch back down the slope. He thought he was going to die; he thought he would never reach the small, slow landing craft that could ferry him a mile or more out to the hospital ships. It was McEldrew's lucky day.

When McEldrew returned to Philadelphia, he learned of the Servicemen's Readjustment Act of 1944, popularly known as the "G.I. Bill of Rights." It provided veterans with stipends that could be used to pay for tuition, books and living expenses. It made college education available to veterans of every income level. Jim McEldrew was the first member of his family to attend college; and when he graduated from college, there was enough benefit remaining to pay for law school. But it was tough to get into a law school. Thousands of war veterans now had the economic wherewithal to meet the pent-up demand for new lawyers. Penn and Temple had no available space, and there were waiting lists for the next three years. McEldrew found an opening in the law school at Rutgers in

New Jersey. After graduation, he returned to Philadelphia and became one of its best-known insurance defense lawyers. The bar was now accessible to people of moderate means. And the G.I. Bill would be reenacted, albeit at lesser levels of educational support, during the Korean and Vietnamese wars.

The judiciary, too, was changing. In 1947, Herbert E. Millen became the first African American on the bench with his appointment to the Philadelphia Municipal Court. Millen had sought that office on five separate occasions beginning in 1935. Four years later, Hannah E. Byrd was appointed to the office of magistrate, becoming the first African-American woman in the minor judiciary. In 1952, Hazel Brown was appointed the first woman judge of the Municipal Court; and from 1954 through 1959 she served as president judge, the position that her father held for thirty-three years. In a reorganization, that court was designated as the "county court," and in 1968 it became the Family Division of the Court of Common Pleas.

Philadelphia was changing. In 1951, a Home Rule Charter was adopted, conferring on the city the authority of self-government including the power to impose taxes. The Charter Commission included Philadelphia lawyers William A. Schnader, Robert T. McCracken, Robert J. Callaghan, Abraham L. Freedman, Thomas B.K. Ringe and Herbert E. Millen. Redevelopment of Philadelphia's historic center was undertaken with the active support of Municipal Court Judge Nochem Winnet and lawyer Walter M. Phillips. The political climate shifted for the first time in a century, and Philadelphia lawyers Richardson Dilworth and Joseph S. Clark were at the crest of the change. Dilworth showed leadership by example when he moved his family from the Rittenhouse Square area into Society Hill, next door to the Athanaeum, the former home of the Law Association. And in Washington, Philadelphia lawyer James P. McGranery was appointed U.S. attorney general, the last Philadelphia lawyer to hold that office in the twentieth century.

As the Philadelphia Bar Association approached its 150th year, its membership was about 2,500 lawyers. Record numbers of law school graduates were entering the legal profession. And the Philadelphia Bar Association elected its first Jewish Chancellor, Bernard G. Segal.

**Coming of Age
(1952-2002)**

On the morning of March 12, 1952, a Red Mass at the Cathedral of Saints Peter and Paul marked the start of the 150th anniversary of the Philadelphia Bar Association. The Saint Thomas More Society of Philadelphia sponsored the event, under the leadership of former Chancellor Walter B. Gibbons. That evening, a formal dinner was held at the Bellevue-Stratford Hotel. The toastmaster was Owen J. Roberts. The principal speaker was George Wharton Pepper. It was "The Last Hurrah" for the Old Philadelphia age of the Association; a new age was coming to birth.

The call went out to all Philadelphia lawyers that they were needed in the Bar Association. When a group of nine local communist leaders was unable to find lawyers to defend them against charges of conspiracy to overthrow the government, a blue-ribbon team of Philadelphia lawyers acting under the auspices of the Bar Association provided the defense. The Association also renewed its efforts in support of an independent judiciary, working to support the "Sitting Judge Principle," which had been in effect since the turn of the century. That principle provided that after a person was appointed or elected to the bench, he or she was then a "sitting judge" whose seat on the court would not be challenged in subsequent elections. In 1953, the Association found it necessary to campaign for the re-election of six sitting judges.

Ten years later, Bernard G. Segal and Jerome J. Shestack took the lead in marshaling support from the legal community for the admission of black students to the University of Alabama. Ultimately, their efforts led to the establishment of the Lawyers' Committee for Civil Rights Under Law, which, in turn, opened an office in Jackson, Mississippi, that was staffed by volunteer lawyers. Philadelphia lawyer William M. Marutani was one of the more interesting volunteers. Marutani is a Nisei, a first generation Japanese-American born in the United States. In 1942, along with 110,000 other Japanese-Americans, he was incarcerated behind barbed wire in the hysteria that followed the Pearl Harbor attack. Later, Marutani served as a commissioned officer in the U.S. Army's historic "Nisei Regiment." In 1983, as a judge of the Court of Common Pleas, he made the decision that required Philadelphia's previously all-male Central High School to admit female students.

Mary Alice Duffy

A new breed of Philadelphia lawyer was entering the scene. In an earlier time, Judges John Innes Clark Hare and Craig Biddle thought women incapable of the toughness required of trial lawyers. It was now too late for Judges Hare and Biddle to preside over a trial handled by Mary Alice Duffy. However, twentieth century judges fell all over themselves trying to avoid confrontations with Mary Alice who, with her sister Sara, started Philadelphia's first all-woman law firm. Lisa Aversa Richette served as an assistant district attorney and wrote on the subject of juvenile justice before assuming a position on the Court of Common Pleas bench. Norma L. Shapiro served a clerkship with Judge

Horace Stern and then practiced in a major Philadelphia law firm, achieving partnership before becoming a judge of the U.S. District Court for the Eastern District of Pennsylvania. In 1979, Dolores K. Sloviter was appointed to the Third Circuit Court of Appeals; a dozen years later, she became the chief judge of that court. Present-day lawyers can scarcely imagine the difficulties faced by the women who practiced law in the 1950s and 1960s when there were virtually no women judges on the bench, no women partners in big law firms and no women executives of major businesses.

In Temple Law School's evening class in the Gimbel's Department Store building at Ninth and Market streets was another new breed of Philadelphia lawyer, Master Sergeant Cecil Bassett Moore. Born and raised in West Virginia, his father was a doctor, his grandfather a minister. Moore was a "Montford Point Marine," a survivor of the special boot camp set up for black Marines at Montford Point in Camp Lejeune, North Carolina. It was a difficult and often denigrating experience. In Philadelphia terms, Montford Point Marines had an "addy-tood." After he was admitted to the bar in 1953, Moore developed an extensive criminal defense practice-and he still had his Montford Point attitude. That was the attitude the public saw when Moore was elected president of Philadelphia's branch of the NAACP in 1962 and when he was on the streets in 1965, leading protests outside Girard College.

Some Philadelphians point to Moore's aggressive protest tactics as the precipitating factor in bringing Girard College back into court. Stephen Girard's school for orphans fared well in the century after Horace Binney's successful defense of the bequest, but there was increasing focus on the testamentary words "poor white male orphans," particularly as the neighborhood surrounding the school became a poor black ghetto. In 1954, African-American lawyers William T. Coleman Jr. and Raymond Pace Alexander filed a petition seeking an order to admit two poor black orphans into Girard College. Similar petitions were filed for the Commonwealth by Attorney General Thomas D. McBride and his deputy Lois G. Forer, and by Abraham L. Freedman for the City of Philadelphia. The case reached the U.S. Supreme Court, which held that the City Board of Trusts, as an agency of the state, could not lawfully discriminate on the basis of race. But on remand, the Orphans' Court appointed private trustees for Girard's estate, and the exclusionary policy remained unchanged. The Supreme Court refused certiorari.

Matters then ground to a halt-until Cecil B. Moore hit the streets. In 1966, William T. Coleman Jr. and Old Philadelphia lawyer Charles J. Biddle petitioned the federal court to order Girard College to admit seven black orphans. The case was assigned to Judge Joseph S. Lord III. On July 5, 1967, Judge Lord granted the petition, and his ruling was affirmed the following year.

In the meanwhile, black Philadelphia lawyers were making significant strides. On two occasions, the Philadelphia Bar Association conducted investigations of alleged racial discrimination in the grading of bar examinations. The first investigation was in 1952 by a special committee, under the leadership of Judge William H. Hastie of the Third Circuit Court of Appeals. The second occurred in 1970 under the leadership of Peter J. Liacouras, then professor of law at Temple Law School. The investigations were inconclusive, but they focused public attention on the unexplained disparity of results in the bar examinations.

In 1955, J. Austin Norris became the senior partner in the firm of Norris, Schmidt, Green, Harris, Higginbotham & Associates. From that firm came Circuit Court of Appeals Judge A. Leon Higginbotham Jr., District Court Judges Clifford Scott Green and Herbert Hutton, U.S. Magistrate Judge William F. Hall Jr., Commonwealth Court Judge

Robert W. Williams Jr., Court of Common Pleas Judges Harvey N. Schmidt and Doris Harris, and chairman of the U.S. Equal Opportunity Commission William H. Brown III.

Clifford Scott Green, William H. Brown, A. Leon Higginbotham, Doris Harris, Austin Norris

In 1958, lawyer Robert N. C. Nix Sr. won a special election for Congress; his son would later become chief justice of the Pennsylvania Supreme Court. In 1959, Juanita Kidd Stout became the first black woman in America to be elected to the bench; she was later appointed to the Pennsylvania Supreme Court. In 1960, Raymond Pace Alexander was elected a judge of the Court of Common Pleas. But it would be another thirty-three years until André L. Dennis was elected as the first African-American Chancellor of the Philadelphia Bar Association.

In the late 1960s, applications to law schools increased. Starting salaries for lawyers increased. Barriers to practicing in suburban counties were lowered with the establishment of a statewide judiciary. And by the start of the 1970s, women accounted for nearly fifty percent of the area's law students. Business corporations increased their in-house law departments. Law firms increased the use of nonlawyer "paralegal" assistants. Duplicating machines almost overnight expanded the ability to communicate and, together with word processing equipment, brought about an end to the use of printed briefs. When personal computers became available in the last decade of the twentieth century, instantaneous global communication was in place, and the world became smaller.

In the meanwhile, the business regulation of the industrial era was relaxed and sometimes eliminated entirely. Businesses that once dominated Philadelphia-Pennsylvania Railroad, Wanamaker's Department Store and Baldwin Locomotive Company, among others-faded from the scene. Competition from the increasing number of lawyers for a decreasing quantity of business created difficult economic circumstances for many lawyers and their firms. Law firms created in the 1920s-era were now in their second or third generation of management, and the relationships between the big firms were no longer like a family.

Mergers and the movement of significant lawyers and groups of lawyers from one firm to another became common. Law firm profitability was an overriding concern. Increasingly, law firms expanded into new geographic areas. Philadelphia's big firms are no longer Philadelphia firms. They are regional, national or even global entities. And there are discussions about the feasibility of multidisciplinary firms.

In a time of territorial expansion of law firms, the Bar Association sustained a significant loss. On July 1, 1967, the Law Library separated from the Philadelphia Bar Association and incorporated as the Theodore F. Jenkins Memorial Law Library, funded under the will of Madeleine Hart Jenkins. That left the Philadelphia Bar Association as the sole remaining entity under the charter originally granted to the Law Library Company in 1802. But the twentieth-century Philadelphia Bar Association was bigger and stronger than ever before. It had a full-time staff and a membership that would grow to more than 14,000 lawyers. The Bar Association had taken on a life of its own.

The Shingle became the official publication of the Association. It provided many Philadelphia lawyers with an outlet for their literary talent. The Shingle came too late for Philadelphia lawyer Owen Wister, who gave up the practice of law at the turn of the century to write the prototype cowboy novel, The Virginian. However, it provided an outlet for the creative talents of later lawyers. From the writings of Common Pleas (and later Pennsylvania Supreme Court) Judge Curtis Bok, Bankruptcy Judge Emil Goldhaber, and U.S. Magistrate Judge Jake Hart, it would appear that a well-honed sense of humor is essential to a career on the bench. Harold Bornemann, who began his career in the law as an office boy in Samuel Dickson's firm, was the institutional memory of the bar. Seymour (Spence) Toll supplied whatever details Bornemann may have forgotten. In 1992, under the guidance of the Association's first woman Chancellor, Deborah R. Willig, the name of the publication was changed to The Philadelphia Lawyer.

Philadelphia lawyers always prided themselves on working together with the judiciary to improve the administration of justice in Philadelphia. New committees, sections and divisions were established within the Bar Association to give effect to the spirit of Philadelphia's lawyers. The Young Lawyers Division, for example, provides a setting for lawyers under 37 years of age. In 1971, Judges Lois G. Forer and Hazel Brown were concerned about an increase in the number of child abuse cases that were coming before the court. They thought that the children were not adequately represented in those hearings and that young lawyers might be able to help. Forer mentioned her concern to young Philadelphia lawyer Marjorie (Meg) Greenfield. Brown discussed it with another young Philadelphia lawyer, James R. Redeker. In June 1971, at the urging of Greenfield and Redeker, the Young Lawyers Section formed a Committee on Child Abuse. The response was immediate. As volunteers and case referrals increased, it became apparent that there would be a continuing need for child advocates. In 1977, the Support Center for Child Advocates was incorporated to continue this important work on a permanent basis. At the present time, the Support Center has a full-time staff, more than 200 volunteers and is representing the interests of more than 500 children each year.

No one needed to tell Philadelphia lawyers that the backlog of civil jury cases had reached an alarming level, often taking between five and six years before cases could be tried. In June 1991, Philadelphia lawyers attracted headlines when forty of the most prominent lawyers volunteered to serve as judges pro tem in an effort to reduce the backlog of civil cases. Two years later, The Wall Street Journal praised those Philadelphia lawyers for the unprecedented degree "to which they've stepped forward to help." But Philadelphia's lawyers were just getting started.

Over the next two years, the Philadelphia Bar Association saw a five-fold increase in the number of volunteer judges pro tem. Starting with new cases filed in 1995, the court implemented a case management program that now brings most cases to trial within eighteen months of the first filing. A key element of the program is the judges pro tem who conduct settlement conferences after the close of discovery. The Dispute Resolution Center, in Room 691, City Hall, prominently displays a plaque containing the names of the judges pro tem and the settlement masters whose volunteer services helped make the program work.

As the Philadelphia Bar Association celebrates its 200th year, change is still in the air just as it was in 1802. The Association no longer has a law library or a finance committee or a committee of censors. But the Association continues to strive for a qualified and independent judiciary, and it continues to evolve to meet the challenges of twenty-first-century law, society and technology. With 13,000 Philadelphia lawyer-members acting through more than fifty committees, eight sections, one division and nearly fifty affiliated organizations, the present-day Philadelphia Bar Association gives new meaning to the traditional term

"Philadelphia lawyer." Present-day Philadelphia lawyers no doubt would agree with Justice Bushrod Washington that "This is my bar." But after a 200-year journey through difficult times, present-day Philadelphia lawyers recognize that, above all, this is our bar.

IV. FICTION

Lawyers deal with facts, as perceived by witnesses and admitted into evidence pursuant to the established rules of courts. Accordingly, it is difficult for lawyers to write about the undocumented thoughts of witnesses and the unspoken intentions of the actors.

On the other hand, the story is much more interesting if it develops the personal predilections of the parties. The following is my first attempt at a fictional account of one of the cases that I handled. Hopefully, you will keep in mind that it is a work of fiction.

A SENIOR WEEK STORY

Cindy looked forward to "senior week" at the New Jersey seashore. It is a tradition in the Philadelphia area that the graduating seniors from local high schools get together with their classmates and rent houses at "the shore" for a week of celebration.

Cindy's high school graduation had been even better than she hoped. Some people thought that she came by success naturally, without effort. They were wrong. Cindy worked hard for everything. It was hard work to earn the leading role in the school play. She was not a born actress. Also, she was not a natural public speaker, but the valedictory address went off without a hitch. Everyone liked her theme of "touching the future." Being offered scholarships at four universities was icing on the cake. In another month, she would pack her things and start a new life at the University of Notre Dame in South Bend, Indiana. But that was next month.

Most of her friends drove to the Jersey shore on Friday, right after the high school graduation. But Cindy stayed home so that she could attend her young cousin's birthday party the following afternoon. She was his godmother. She knew that the birthday was important to the youngster, and she knew that senior week would still be there at the shore for another six days. So she postponed her own celebration, and stayed home for the birthday party. Cindy was like that.

It was late Saturday evening when Cindy finally left home to join the senior week festivities. She took the

Atlantic City Expressway east to the Garden State Parkway, and then south to Sea Isle City. It was far later than she had expected to arrive at the shore. She now regretted having promised to stop and see the house that Tommy Kehner and his friends rented in Strathmere. But it was important to Cindy that her first senior week stop be at Tommy's house. She had planned every step of this week for the past three months, ever since she received the scholarship from Notre Dame.

Cindy and Tommy had been going together for nearly two years. They began to date shortly after Tommy invited her to the junior prom. After that, they were always together. Everyone took it for granted that they would be married. The only question was when? Cindy knew that four years at Notre Dame was a long time to be away from anyone. It was the chance of a lifetime; and when she graduated from Notre Dame, who knows what opportunities would be available? And where? After four years of college, she would be a different person. She thought it through and decided to break off her relationship with Tommy before she left for college.

She planned to raise the subject during the course of senior week, and to complete the break in the weeks that followed. It would be low key at the start. Whenever someone in the group mentioned a memorable instance from their high school days, Cindy planned to speculate on a similar activity at Notre Dame, particularly the football games. It would be a gradual process and hopefully Tommy would agree that breaking up was a good thing to do under the circumstances. In the meanwhile, Cindy wanted to set the stage for these discussions by showing that a visit to Tommy's seashore house was for her a matter of first importance.

As she drove along the causeway into Sea Isle City, Cindy wondered whether she should give up the idea of starting the plan with a visit to Tommy's place. Would it really make a difference? Cindy wrestled with the thought until she crossed the causeway and reached Landis Avenue, the Ocean Drive. A right turn would take her to the house that she had rented with her friends. It was time for a decision. She turned to the left and headed north to the edge of Strathmere, some two and one-half miles distant.

This part of Strathmere is little more than a long, straight stretch of road separating the ocean from the bay. A short distance to the north, a small bridge connects Strathmere to the south end of Ocean City. Tommy's house was about a quarter-mile before the bridge. Cindy parked on the undeveloped ocean side of the highway. On the left side of the road, only one house had its lights on. It was the right place. Tommy Kehner and his friends were delighted that Cindy kept her promise to make their Strathmere house her first senior week stop. For her part, Cindy regretted taking the can of beer that they pressed on her upon her arrival. It was like a ceremonial toast, like the Olympic flame; it launched the senior week – a once in a lifetime celebration. She did not want the beer but she took it anyway and tried to ignore the upset in her stomach. Everyone gathered in the kitchen. They reveled in reliving the events of their first day of senior week.

Cindy was tired. She walked into the front room to relax. It was nearly 2:30 in the morning. There was an ocean chill in the sparsely furnished seashore living room. Cindy felt a shiver run through her and pulled the wool sweater closer around her shoulders. She reached for a cigarette but then remembered that they were still in her car.

Six miles south of Strathmere, Jim Callahan fumbled with the change in his pocket as he drove up to the toll bridge between Avalon and Townsends Inlet. It had been a great day, just like the good times in Boulder, Colorado. Jim was stationed in Boulder while in the army. Boulder is a college town. The coeds were pretty and liked a good time. Jim had money in his pocket and plenty of time on his hands. The college students were impressed that he had been to Europe. They thought that Jim was sophisticated and interesting. The European experience gave him a talking point to exploit. He called himself a college student, temporarily in the army. He would finish his studies after his discharge — so the story went. The story was like a fine wine; it got better with age. Jim had no intention of attending college. He was better than the people he met at the local watering holes. School was a drag.

And so were those Colorado policemen a drag. When he was tagged with his second DUI conviction, Jim decided that it was time to take a discharge from the army and drive back to the east coast. He knew a coed who wanted to go back home to Philadelphia, and he talked Karen into sharing the drive with him. The trip was uneventful. After a few weeks working as a mechanic in New Brunswick, New Jersey, Jim missed the good times that he had in Boulder. He called Karen and promised to meet her in Ocean City where she was now staying at her parents' summer house while working as a waitress. Jim borrowed his father's station wagon for the trip.

Home turned out not to be the place that Karen had in mind when she dropped out of college. She expected to find a place that no longer existed. Her friends from high school were scattered in a number of different places. Some were away at distant colleges. Others were immersed in their new lives at local colleges. Some were working full time. Gone was the camaraderie that she once enjoyed. Karen's parents viewed her return with mixed emotions. They were glad to have her back home, but they would rather that she had transferred to a local school. In the meanwhile, Karen's mother insisted that Karen get a full-time job. They compromised. Karen moved into the family's Ocean City house, and promised to get a job at the seashore until she was ready to return to school. Karen had forgotten how dull Ocean City was in the off-season. She was glad to see Jim.

Together, Jim and Karen drove to a liquor store at the circle in Somers Point where they picked up a bottle of vodka and a six-pack of German beer. Then, they went back to Karen's place by the beach. There, they toasted the good times that they shared in Boulder. After a few drinks, Karen suggested that they drive down to Avalon and meet her friend Marie McMahon. Karen and Marie were a lot alike. They had been friends since high school in the Philadelphia suburbs. Like Karen, Marie had dropped out of college and was living in her parents' summer house. Marie was pretty. She had dark brown hair and a friendly smile. Jim liked her immediately. They sat in Marie's kitchen, drinking German beer and swapping stories about Boulder and Avalon. Marie suggested that they drive over to the Princeton Hotel, which was one of the gathering spots for the twenty-somethings in Avalon. It was early in the season. When they arrived at the Princeton, very few people were there. After a drink at the bar, one of the girls – Jim could not recall which one – suggested that they try Ralph's Tavern in Stone Harbor.

Stone Harbor is an affluent seashore community that adjoins Avalon to the south. Ralph's is located on the main commercial street that runs at a ninety-degree angle to the Ocean Drive. Jim pulled his car around to the back of the building where there is a large parking lot. The bar was crowded. Karen and Marie seemed to know everyone, and everyone accepted Jim as one of the crowd. It was not long before Jim announced that he was switching his drink to schnapps because that was what he drank when he was in Germany. The girls were impressed. It was Boulder all over again. The good times rolled with schnapps until the bartender announced "last call" and Jim noticed that it was almost 2:00 a.m. The crowd had thinned out. Marie had gone home with one of her friends. Karen was ready to go home. She would have a tough time staying awake on the drive back to Ocean City. As soon as Jim started the car, Karen turned on the heater. The warm air made her even drowsier.

Cindy shivered as she stepped out of the front door of the house in Strathmere. Her car was parked across the street on the ocean side of the two-lane Ocean Drive. It was starting to rain. As Cindy walked across the choppy weed-like grass in front of the house, she glanced to her right and saw headlights far in the distance. Looking back toward her car, she let her mind wander, thinking about her own rental house in Sea Isle City, unpacking and getting some sleep. She would have just one cigarette and then be on her way. She would meet up with the boys in the morning after the 11:00 a.m. Mass in Sea Isle.

Cindy was just a few feet from her car when she was blinded by the glare of headlights from her right. "My God!" she exclaimed, "So fast!" Cindy pivoted to her left, but it was too late.

Karen slouched uncomfortably on the front seat of Jim's station wagon. Her eyes were closed and she dozed off and on. At one point, her eyes opened slightly and swept sleepily across the instrument panel. With a start, she saw the speed indicator move past the 70 mph mark. She started to tell Jim to slow down when she looked through the windshield and involuntarily screamed. Karen's scream jolted Jim awake. There was a girl directly in front of the car. It looked like she was standing still. Where did she come from? Jim slammed the brake pedal to the floor. At almost the same instant, there was a sickening thud, followed by a crunching impact on the windshield directly in front of Karen. The station wagon skidded to a stop. Jim and Karen opened the doors and got out of the car. It was drizzling rain. It was dark. It was eerily quiet. A light in a house across the street was the only sign of life. Twenty feet behind the station wagon, a girl was lying on the road. There was hardly a mark on her. It looked like she was asleep; but she was not breathing. Karen and Jim were in a state of shock. They were like two statues standing in the middle of the road when another car came along and someone called the police.

The next few hours passed by as though in a dream – a bad dream. Jim had dreamed this dream before. Flashing red and blue emergency lights, bright floodlights, popping flashbulbs, snapping of camera lenses, and the smartly creased uniforms of three different police departments blended together as evidence was collected for official records. Jim and Karen were placed in the back of a squad car and hustled off to the State Police Barracks at Port Norris. At the barracks, the questioning started. Again and again they repeated what had happened, and where they had been earlier in the day. Would they consent to the taking of blood samples? Karen was terrified. She could not understand what was happening. Why was she being treated like a criminal? She did not drive the car; she was a passenger. Her parents would be mortified. She dreaded facing them. Karen lashed out at the police officers, spewing obscenities like a member of a motorcycle gang. Much to her chagrin, Karen's abusive conduct only increased the suspicions of the officers. Maybe she had been the driver of the station wagon. The questions became more hostile.

In the meanwhile, Jim was numb. His brain was numb. His blood alcohol content was 0.175%, well above the legal driving limit of 0.10%. His brain may not have been functioning properly, but Jim knew what was happening. He had been in police custody before. The station wagon was quickly traced to Jim's father. A check with the nationwide police network brought to light the two prior DUI convictions in Colorado and the automatic suspension of his driving privileges. It was Boulder all over again – but this time the police were using the word "homicide." The girl on the road was dead.

In Rydal, Pennsylvania, just northwest of Philadelphia, Jeanne and Fritz Koehler were sleeping a fitful sleep. Rydal is one of those Levittown-like bedroom communities of pre-cut housing that sprang up outside Philadelphia in the 1950s. Families that lived in the "river wards" of Philadelphia, the neighborhoods that stretch north along the Delaware River, migrated across the city line into Montgomery and Bucks Counties. Rydal is in Montgomery County.

Jeanne and Fritz grew up in a Philadelphia neighborhood near the Frankford railroad yards and the Port Richmond coal piers. The German nuns at Our Lady Help of Christians Church dubbed young Francis X. Koehler "Fritz" – and the name stuck. During his high school years, Fritz had a part-time job in a nearby factory. Fritz had a good head on his shoulders. He worked in the factory office, helping to keep the company's accounting records. It matured into a full-time job after his graduation from North Catholic High School. Not long after they were married, Jeanne and Fritz jumped at the chance to join the exodus out of the old industrial neighborhood and into suburbia. The new house was not that much larger, but the layout was more convenient, the windows let in light and air from all sides of the house, and there was a yard with real grass. Also, there were no noxious odors from rendering plants along the railroad tracks.

The years had taken a toll on Fritz. Like most of the employees at the plant, Fritz thought that the fuss about asbestos would go away. But it did not go away. Being in the accounting office, Fritz was quick to understand that sales had slowed to a trickle. Then the lawsuits started. The company "tightened its belt." There were layoffs. Part of the factory was shut down. The accounting office was among the last to go. Last year, Fritz received a termination notice. Jobs were scarce. The economic pressure of unemployment was unbearable. Fritz felt as though he was losing his mind. Then he fell down the stairs in his house. He just blacked out for a moment, and the next thing he knew his head hit the living room floor. What was happening? It seemed like fate was plotting against him.

Cindy's high school graduation was a welcome relief. Fritz envied his daughter and her friends. When he was in high school there was no "senior week." There was no class trip. There was no elaborate celebration. There was only the factory. Deep down inside, Fritz wished that he was back in his senior year at North Catholic looking forward to a week in Wildwood, New Jersey with his old neighborhood crowd.

Jeanne doted on the four children, shepherding them through each day from breakfast to bedtime. In between she worked in the office of the parish school. It did not pay much but Jeanne enjoyed being around the school children and any little bit of money helped, especially with Fritz being out of work. She was glad that the graduation was over. It was wonderful that Cindy did so well but Jeanne was not really comfortable with all of the attention that the family received over the past few weeks.

Jeanne also was not too comfortable with the idea of senior week. She would have preferred that Cindy and her friends stayed home and celebrated in the neighborhood. But Cindy was almost on her own now. The college years were about to begin. They were a good group of kids. Jeanne knew that she could not stand in the way of senior week. But that did not keep her from worrying about it.

The first rays of sunlight were just starting to appear when Fritz and Jeanne realized that the repeated ringing was their doorbell and not a dream. Jeanne went to the window and looked out. There was a State Police car parked at the curb. The officer apologized for waking them at that hour but said that it was important. He had bad news. It was a very difficult way to learn that their oldest daughter was dead. At that moment, part of Fritz and Jeanne Koehler died too. But there were three other children asleep in their bedrooms. Fritz and Jeanne could not allow themselves the luxury of losing control.

Hardly had the sun risen over the scene of the accident when the lawyers began to gather. Sketchy details of the accident were reported in the morning radio and television news shows. Philadelphia lawyers with summer homes in Strathmere decided that it was a nice morning for a walk along the Ocean Drive where State Police photographers were still recording the accident scene for their investigation files. Who knows, someone at the scene might have a question about legal liability for the accident. Lawyers with offices in Cape May County wrote letters to Jeanne and Fritz, telling them about past efforts to improve the lighting on the Ocean Drive, and offering to be of assistance to them. Owners of drinking establishments from Wildwood to Strathmere huddled together and prayed that the driver of that station wagon had not been a patron in their establishments on Saturday night.

Jeanne Koehler's sister Janet was Cindy's godmother. Janet worked for one of the best law firms in Philadelphia. She was the personal secretary to Kendall Johnson, an expert in the intricacies of administrative law. Personal injury litigation was not Johnson's specialty but he promised to arrange for a favorable fee agreement and to have the claim handled by one of the firm's best trial lawyers. The typical Philadelphia legal fee contract for personal injury cases is a one-third contingency contract. That means that there is no fee unless the lawyer achieves a recovery for the client and, in that case, the fee is one-third of the recovery. Johnson proposed a fee arrangement that provided for a fee based on an hourly rate in the event that the claim was settled within five weeks, but a one-third contingency if the matter required a longer period of time. It was an arrangement favorable to the Koehlers because it would be unlikely that the hourly charges for five weeks would even approach one-third of a settlement figure.

The following week, Jeanne and Fritz Koehler went to center city Philadelphia, and met with the trial lawyer, Johnson's partner Gregory David Gushue. The Koehlers tried to follow what Mr. Gushue was telling them, but it was difficult. Jeanne and Fritz struggled with the tumultuous mixture of pride in achievement and finality in death. The picture in the newspaper was so clear, so lifelike. Cindy was at the podium speaking about touching the future and anticipating a bright future at Notre Dame University. And there was the casket and the Mass of the Resurrection, and the bill for the funeral. Who would have thought that a funeral would cost so much? Fritz's eyes, red and watery, showed the strain. "We'll get through it. We'll get on with our lives. I don't want to think about suing someone." Jeanne looked up and her eyes conveyed the same message but she regained her composure and she said, "Tell us what we should do."

Gushue explained the basic principles of negligence law. The driver of an automobile is responsible for any damage caused by his negligent acts. It sounded simple enough at first but then but the word "damage" and the repeated references to responsibility for "amounts" made it sound as though Cindy's life could be reduced to a dollars-and-cents price list. Gushue was well aware that civil juries can only award verdicts in dollars and cents. There are no schedules or formulas by which to measure a life. It is up to each jury to determine what amount of money is appropriate to redress the injury caused by a negligent driver. All fifty states adhere to these general principles of law.

However, Pennsylvania and New Jersey apply the principles differently. Pennsylvania's measure takes into account the entire lifetime of the victim's probable future earnings whereas New Jersey allows recovery of only that part of the victim's probable lifetime earnings that family members reasonably could have expected to receive had the victim survived. New Jersey's measure results in a much smaller number. And New Jersey law would probably be applied to this case because the drinking, the driving, the accident and the death all occurred in New Jersey. Another complication was that Jim, the person who caused the fatality, was not in a position to assume any financial responsibility whatever. He was broke. But he was driving his father's car and his father had a total of $300,000 insurance coverage that could be applied to Jim's liability.

Greg Gushue uneasily sensed that the conversation was drifting dangerously close to the proposition that the law measures lives in monetary terms, and that lawyers are interested only in getting a share of those dollars and cents for themselves. Nothing could be farther from the truth. Greg found it easy to identify with Fritz and Jeanne. His father's family lived in the same Philadelphia neighborhood where Fritz and Jeanne grew up. They had mutual acquaintances. And Gushue's oldest daughter just graduated from high school and was celebrating senior week in Wildwood the night that Cindy was killed. In fact, when he heard the sketchy early morning reports of the incident, Greg worried that his daughter might have been involved – either as the victim or the driver. He knew the concerns of parents when their children want to go to the seashore for a week after graduation. And he could understand the questions that parents invariably have when celebration times turn to tragedy.

Gushue leaned back in his chair, gathering his thoughts on how to explain an adversarial legal system that pits one party against another in a search for truth; and measures the result in dollars and cents. The thought of adversaries pitted against each other brought back an old memory of hand-to-hand combat exercises in boot camp. It was years since his officer candidate experience in Quantico, Virginia, but the recollection was clear. He smiled at the memory. The drill instructor said that there might come a time when you suddenly are knocked down or fall backward off your feet and are likely to be hurt when you hit the ground. Basic physics teaches that an impact will be distributed with less effect if the force is spread out over a large area. They taught the recruits to swing their arms backward and slap the ground, spreading out the impact down the length of their arms and shoulders. Now, leaning forward toward Fritz and Jeanne, Greg explained that the law acts in the same way to spread out the impact of Cindy's death so that the loss is shared by everyone who played a part in bringing it about. As he reflected on his own words, Gushue liked the explanation. He made a mental note to use it in other cases.

Jeanne wanted to know whether there were any other persons besides Jim who might share the responsibility for Cindy's death. Gushue did not yet have all of the facts of the accident but said that one distinct possibility was that someone might have been negligent in serving alcohol to Jim. In that case, it would have to be proved that the server knew or should have known that Jim was intoxicated at the time he was served – a tough hurdle. Hopefully, the police investigation would identify where Jim was during the evening and early morning hours before the accident. Once the drinking spot was identified, Gushue could interview witnesses to determine the facts that would allow him to evaluate the potential liability of other persons.

In Cape May Court House, the county prosecutor sat at his desk and looked alternately at a new file folder and at the young assistant sitting across from him. It was a high profile case. Already newspaper reporters and television networks were calling his office wanting to know the details about the charges that would be brought in the case of the "senior week" fatality. For the time being, he told them that the matter would be submitted to the September grand jury. The grand jury would make the determination whether or not the driver would be charged with homicide by auto. It would be a difficult hearing. The prosecution would be required to present evidence that Jim was grossly negligent, i.e., negligence to the extent that it amounted to criminal intent. The blood alcohol content of 0.175% was proof of negligence but the prosecutor would need more.

Except for the driver and his passenger, there were no witnesses to the occurrence. There was no way that the driver would testify. He would exercise his Fifth Amendment right to remain silent. "That bitch who was with him won't be any help," said the older man. Charlie Patton, the young assistant had been with the prosecutor's office for less than a year. This case called for more experience, but there was no one else. Oh well, everyone has to start somewhere. "What do you think, Charlie," said the older man, "do you think that you can take this one to the grand jury?" "No problem," Charlie replied.

The grand jury is a longstanding part of the common law. A grand jury is "grand" in the sense that it is larger than the familiar twelve-person jury, which is called a petit or "petty" jury. A grand jury usually consists of sixteen or more persons. In cases like the senior week death it is used to determine whether the evidence warrants criminal charges against the accused. The grand jury hears only the state's evidence and decides whether that evidence, standing alone, establishes that the defendant committed the crime. If the evidence is sufficient, the grand jury returns an "indictment," which is the criminal complaint against the defendant. If no indictment is returned, there will be no criminal prosecution but only a traffic court charge of driving under the influence. The assistant prosecutor will ask the grand jury to return an indictment charging Jim with criminal homicide, death by automobile, a crime that is punishable by more than five years imprisonment.

The county prosecutor tried to stay out of the way of his young assistant. During most of the grand jury proceeding, he would linger in the back of the courtroom where it would not appear as though he was directing the action, and he would frequently leave the room and go back to his office to catch up on paperwork. No one other than the prosecutors, the witness who is testifying and the grand jurors are allowed in the courtroom. The grand jury proceeding is cloaked in secrecy. It was not long before the prosecutor wondered whether he was making a mistake by watching the sessions. It was not going well. He found himself twisting his hands on his lap, trying to restrain himself from jumping up and taking over the questioning. If he did that, the young assistant would never learn to handle a grand jury and the office would be weaker in the long run. He would just have to suffer in silence and try to offer helpful suggestions afterwards.

Both of the state troopers were good witnesses. Officer Pettit had been the first on the scene. He took over from the Sea Isle City Police. He looked like a professional football player. Referring to his typewritten report, he rattled off the details of time, place and distance in a military manner. Each fact was precisely stated. Corporal Tobolsh presented a contrast in appearance. He was short and slender, and his hairline was receding markedly. Tobolsh had interrogated the accused and supervised the blood alcohol tests. His testimony was also to the point and precise. That's the problem, thought the old prosecutor, everything is cut and dried. The impact was forty-four feet from the intersection, three feet from the shoulder of the road, at exactly 2:43 a.m. Even the blood alcohol percentage was recited to the third decimal place. The grand jury is going to lose sight of the fact that a girl died. An experienced prosecutor would know how to keep the focus on reality but, when you are still learning the ropes, it is sometimes impossible to create the necessary atmosphere in the courtroom.

The grand jury instinctively picked up on the absence of urgency in the testimony. They were not "summer people." The grand jurors were selected from the voting rolls of Cape May County. Most of the jurors lived in remote locations and worked in the light construction or service jobs that proliferate in seashore communities. Local drinking spots are their social centers. If they did not drive with blood alcohol in excess of the legal limit, some of them would never get home at night. They would hold a drunk driver responsible for a death caused in an automobile accident but more often than not it would be a traffic offense and not a homicide charge – unless there was some clear element of recklessness or malice. And that is how they understood the judge's instructions. The way they saw it was that Callahan drove more than twelve miles, through Stone Harbor, Avalon, Townsends Inlet, Sea Isle City, and Strathmere, and across a narrow toll bridge, paying a live toll collector. The accident occurred at an unlighted location and the station wagon was in the proper lane for northbound traffic. The police had plenty of opportunity to locate witnesses if Jim's conduct had been reckless, but no one testified that he drove recklessly. The grand jury decided not to return an indictment.

Charlie Patton took the decision hard. He would get over it. However, for the present he blamed the grand jurors. Conversely, the lawyer hired by Jim's parents was ecstatic. Jim's parents were relieved. But Jim could not muster up any enthusiasm. He knew that the matter would now be sent to traffic court and that his prior record of DUI offenses in Colorado would be likely to result in jail time. He called one of his army buddies to see whether he was serious when he said that it would be easy to assume a new identity in some parts of New York City.

The Cape May County Prosecutor sent Fritz and Jeanne a perfunctory letter, informing them of the grand jury's determination and stating that the DUI proceeding was to be scheduled by a district judge in Upper Township. Ironically, the letter also advised them that victims have the right to hire a private attorney at their own expense to prosecute the DUI violation. Such a right does not exist at the grand jury level. The victim plays no part in the criminal justice process.

In the meanwhile, Gregory Gushue received copies of the police files on Cindy's death. The files included an accident report, photos of the scene taken shortly after the accident and a set taken later in the day, medical reports, an autopsy report and statements and identification of persons interviewed. Significantly, the file included the name and Ocean City address and phone number of Karen Thompson, the passenger in Jim's car. It also identified Ralph's Tavern in Stone Harbor as the place from which Jim began his drive north to Strathmere.

Greg immediately placed a call to Karen Thompson in Ocean City. There was no answer. He left a message on the recording machine, asking Karen to return his call. Before he left the office that evening, he placed another call with the same result. The following afternoon, he placed another call – and a female voice answered the phone. It was Karen. Gushue identified himself and said that he would like to meet with her to discuss the senior week accident. Somewhat reluctantly, Karen said that she would like to cooperate with Cindy's family but she was not sure when such a meeting could be arranged. Gushue volunteered to drive to Ocean City and be there within two hours. Karen agreed to meet him at a lemonade stand in the south part of Ocean City. Gushue canceled his afternoon appointments, rented a car and drove directly to Ocean City.

It was a cool afternoon. The lemonade stand was closed. Gushue got out of his car and walked over to one of the benches that surrounded the lemonade business. It was not long before Karen arrived. She had light colored hair and was in her early twenties. Greg asked whether she would prefer to talk at an indoor location such as one of the restaurants in the center of town. Karen was satisfied with the present location, and sat down on one of the benches.

Greg sat down beside her and asked about her home and where she went to school. He was accustomed to interviewing witnesses, and soon switched the conversation from Karen's family to the day of the accident. They talked about Jim and Boulder, Colorado, and the drive back to the east coast. Karen described in detail Jim's visit to the Jersey shore on the afternoon before the accident, and the drive to Avalon and Stone Harbor. Greg had a note pad and a pen but he rarely made a note. He would listen hard to what Karen said, and then make detailed notes from memory after the meeting was over. They talked for nearly an hour. Karen assured Greg that she would be available to testify at a deposition. She said that she would try to convince her friend Marie to cooperate with the Koehlers. She declined Greg's offer to drive her back to her parents' house, but said that she was glad that she had the opportunity to discuss the incident. Karen felt terrible about being so close to a tragedy and being so afraid to talk about it to anyone. She thanked Mr. Gushue for listening to her. Greg wondered whether that is what a priest feels like after hearing a confession.

Back in his car, Gushue pulled out his notepad and hurriedly wrote detailed notes about the conversation that just ended. He placed instinctive emphasis on the drinking that occurred before Jim and Karen arrived at Ralph's Tavern, and the time of arrival and the estimated amount of alcohol consumed while there. If a complaint was to be filed against Ralph's, it would be premised on those facts. Karen's story raised the possibility that Jim's inebriation occurred well before his arrival at Ralph's. If that was the case, should Ralph's have noticed Jim's inebriated condition? That would be a key aspect of any claim against the tavern. Additional investigation was necessary but Gregory David Gushue now felt that he had enough information to advise Fritz and Jeanne on a legal course of action.

As Gushue expected, the company that insured Callahan's father offered the full policy limits of $300,000 to settle the Koehlers' claim against Jim. Such a settlement and the inevitable general release would extinguish any further claims by the Koehlers against Jim and his parents. That would be an acceptable trade-off because Jim was penniless and there were no known facts that would warrant a direct claim against his parents. The Koehlers authorized Gushue to accept the policy limits offer. At the same time, the Koehlers asked Gushue exactly how much of the $300,000 they would receive. Greg did not have an immediate answer to that question. He would have to check it out with the firm's management and accounting people. He told Fritz and Jeanne that he would have an answer for them the following day. In the meanwhile, he asked Fritz and Jeanne to give thought to how they would like to receive the funds. They planned to discuss that with a close friend who worked as an administrator at Cindy's high school.

The insurance company's policy limits offer created a problem for Gregory Gushue. He did not own the law firm. He was just a mid-level partner. Moreover, the Koehlers were not his clients; they were considered to be the clients of the more senior lawyer Kendall Johnson. Three months had passed since the contingent fee contract was signed. For a settlement within the first five weeks, the fee would be charged on an hourly basis, in which case the fee would be $30,000. However, more than three months had passed and, under those circumstances, the one-third contingency came into play warranting a fee of $100,000. Gushue met with his partner Johnson, and recommended that the firm's fee be set at $30,000, plus reimbursement of the firm's out-of-pocket costs. He said that the passage of time beyond five-weeks was the result of systemic delays that were not caused by either the firm or the clients. The firm would be paid in full for the work at its usual fee level, and there would be another opportunity for a contingent fee in connection with the dram shop claim against Ralph's Tavern. Also, the clients were close family members of a valued employee of the firm, and they had an obvious need for the money. Johnson agreed, and promised to take up the matter with the firm's executive committee. That evening, the executive committee approved a fee of $30,000.

Gushue was happy with the result but he knew that some members of the executive committee probably opposed the reduced fee. Those persons would view $100,000 as their personal property; and the way they would see it was that Gushue gave away $70,000 of their money. Such persons tend to have long memories. Moreover, as members of the law firm's executive committee, they were in a position to wield significant power. The executive committee determines each lawyer's annual compensation and bonuses. It assigns client responsibilities. And it does most of its important work behind closed doors. Gushue suspected that he might feel the effects of this fee recommendation in years to come.

The Koehlers were delighted with the firm's decision. It meant that they were entitled to receive an immediate payment of almost $270,000. Among trial lawyers, there is a rule of thumb that plaintiffs who receive large monetary awards usually dissipate that money within three years. Apparently, the Koehlers' advisor knew of that rule of thumb because Fritz and Jeanne said that they would take $250,000 in the form of a structured settlement. In a structured settlement, part of the settlement money is used to purchase an annuity contract from an insurance carrier or other financial institution. The annuity then pays out money to the settlers in accordance with the terms of the contract. The Koehlers' broker worked out an annuity that would pay a lifetime monthly income of about $2,000, plus ten lump-sum payments that averaged $34,000, which would be paid at three-year intervals and would help meet college expenses for the remaining three children. Best yet, all of these payments would be exempt from federal income tax. The balance of $20,000 would be used to pay the funeral bill, the law firm's costs, and to meet immediate family needs. Gushue contacted the Lambertville Insurance Company and requested two checks, one payable to the annuity company in the amount of $250,000, and the other payable to the Koehlers and the law firm in the amount of $50,000.

A few days later, Greg received a call from the claims adjuster of the Lambertville Insurance Company, stating that he had the checks in hand and would put them in the mail. Then the adjuster said, "Wait a minute, my branch manager wants to talk to you." An authoritative voice came on the line and said, "Mr. Gushue, I just want to ask whether this check in the amount of $50,000 includes your firm's legal fees. Does it?" When Greg responded in the affirmative, the voice on the other end of the line said, "Mr. Gushue, I don't usually see a fee this low for a $300,000 settlement. I would like to shake your hand."

In the meanwhile, Jim's DUI case was called for trial in the Township of Upper, west of the bay. When the court clerk called the case, Jim was not there. He had picked up stakes and moved out of his parents' home. He left no forwarding address. A rumor circulated that he was in New York but no one knew exactly where he was. It was more than a year later that he reluctantly notified the authorities that he wanted to return and bring the proceeding to an end. He then pleaded guilty to the charges.

On the day that Jim was to be sentenced, the courtroom was packed. Most of the persons present in court were there to argue their own cases involving minor traffic infractions. It was a noisy crowd. A hush fell over the courtroom when Jeanne was asked by the Judge to make a statement on behalf of the victim's family. Jeanne spoke of her hopes and dreams and then of the doorbell ringing early that Sunday morning and the conversation with the state policeman. It was simple, and eloquent, and moving. After considering the case for about an hour, the judge suspended Jim's driver's license for two years and sentenced him to 90 days in jail, 30 days community service and participation in an alcohol recovery program. Gregory Gushue thought that the sentence was hardly enough for such a tragic crime but it was the inevitable result of the grand jury's refusal to issue an indictment. You do not always get your way in the law.

Gushue would have preferred to file a complaint against Ralph's Tavern in the federal district court in Philadelphia. A venue in Pennsylvania would have given him an opportunity to argue for the application of the much more favorable law of Pennsylvania. However, there was no legitimate way to serve Pennsylvania process on a tavern that is located 75 miles outside the border of the state. And so it was that suit was filed in federal court in the District of New Jersey in Camden. Ironically, the Camden courthouse is just across the Delaware River – barely a mile from the federal courthouse in Philadelphia. On the Lindenwold High-Speed Transit Line the two courthouses are just two stops apart.

The case was assigned to a newly appointed Judge Manuel Montoya, who quickly scheduled a conference of counsel to establish a case management schedule. As Greg Gushue emerged from the subway station, the drab neighborhood and the backdrop of the Campbell's Soup Company factories signaled to Greg that he was an outsider. The federal courthouse is an austere building. A dingy coffee shop and a few tired retail businesses occupied the ground level. It did not get any better when the elevator deposited Gushue on the second floor. The conference room was a bare-bones affair with none of the amenities that characterized the federal courthouses in Philadelphia, New York City and Washington, D.C. On the other hand, Judge Manuel Montoya was the genuine article. He was all business. He wanted to know what the case was about and how the parties intended to present their claims and defenses. After listening to the responses of the lawyers for both sides, Judge Montoya allowed six months for discovery procedures, after which the case would be brought to trial. What with the police reports already in hand, and the interview of Karen completed, six months was plenty of time.

The facts in hand showed that Jim came to Ocean City intent on imbibing a significant quantity of alcohol, and that he pursued that goal from the beginning. After his arrival at Ralph's Tavern, the evidence showed that he continued to drink. The police record established that Jim's blood alcohol content was 0.175% shortly after the accident. The sympathy of the jury would be with Cindy's family. But this was a court of law. Gushue needed evidence, not sympathy. He needed evidence that the employees of Ralph's Tavern either knew or should have known that Jim was intoxicated while they continued to serve him alcohol. Without that type of evidence, a jury might reject the claim of liability against the tavern – just as the grand jury declined to return an indictment. The case against the tavern needed to be reinforced – but how?

Despite his facade of cool indifference, Gushue was a worrywart. He mentally replayed the anticipated testimony of the police officers, Karen and Marie over and over again. It did not satisfy him. He had represented taverns before in similar cases. He had prepared tavern owners just like Ralph to testify at depositions. Typically, tavern owners are on the premises for some amount of time every night the bar is open. Although most owners will not admit it, the fact is that they are there mainly to keep an eye on the bartenders and any other employee with access to the cash register. The bar business is tough enough without trusted employees pocketing money or otherwise giving away the store. Depositions of tavern owners are usually taken several years after the event in question. Moreover, the event did not happen in the bar; it happened on a highway miles away. The tavern owner did not find out about it until much later. Under those circumstances, it is almost impossible for anyone to recall the events in the bar with any degree of certainty.

Undoubtedly, Ralph would testify that he was probably present in the tavern on that Saturday night, but that he had no specific recollection of any particular details of the business that evening. He does not know Jim Callahan and cannot recall ever seeing anyone by that name in the place. Although he often hears the names "Karen" and "Marie," he does not know Karen Thompson or Marie McMahon. It is a pretty good bet that he will also volunteer that he is sorry that he cannot be more helpful. That testimony is not helpful at all. More evidence was needed.

Gushue put his mind on "automatic pilot." The question continually hovered in his mind, albeit at a subconscious level. The unanswered question was still there one morning as he sat at the breakfast table. He picked up the newspaper and went right to the local section to review the death notices, which he called the "Irish Comics." There it was on the front page of the local section – his answer.

It was a story about a popular tavern in the Main Line area. The tavern required its bartenders and cocktail waitresses to attend a course of training on intervention procedures designed to identify patrons who were in danger of consuming too much alcohol and to assure that corrective measures were taken. Instantly, the mental file on the suit against Ralph's opened and began to interact with the information in the article. Within an hour he had a telephone number for the Washington, D.C. office of the organization that presented the program described in the newspaper. He dialed that number.

As the phone rang, Gushue mentally practiced what he would say when a voice answered at the other end of the line. It was not difficult at all because the man on the other end of the line immediately understood the problem. He too was a lawyer. His name was Adam. He was the vice president of a nonprofit corporation that promoted intervention procedures to be used by establishments that sold alcoholic beverages. His father founded the company. The father was a psychiatrist associated with the Harvard medical school. He founded the nonprofit corporation to deal with a growing problem in this country. Adam said that he knew the reputation of Gushue's law firm. He had been an associate in the Washington D.C. office of the Philadelphia firm of Wolf, Block, Schorr & Solis-Cohen, a firm that was located just a few floors below Gushue's firm in Philadelphia's Packard Building. Although it was not a part of the nonprofit's operations to testify in litigation, Adam gave Greg the name and phone number of Nancy Coolican, a certified intervention instructor who might be able to help in that regard.

Nancy was indeed helpful. She described what the tavern servers should do to avoid intoxication of their patrons. In the first instance, they should engage the patron in conversation, and listen carefully to the customer's speech. Are the words slurred? Do they make sense? Look directly into their eyes; are they bloodshot? The server should keep track of what the customer has consumed. They should mentally calculate the alcohol content. Switching drinks is often a warning sign of approaching intoxication. The server should always deal with the customer face-to-face. Servers should beware of the situation where one customer buys "a round" for a group of other customers whom the server cannot evaluate. Similarly, a bartender should not serve people who are standing two or three deep at the bar who cannot be closely observed. Nancy's comments highlighted the factors that Gushue should try to elicit from the witnesses whose testimony would be taken at deposition. Nancy said that once she had a complete file on the matter, she could send Greg a report of her evaluation of the situation at Ralph's Tavern, including her opinion as to whether or not Ralph's actions were negligent.

Shortly after this discussion, Gushue scheduled the deposition testimony of Karen Thompson and Marie McMahon to take place in a lawyer's office in Atlantic City, New Jersey. Karen lived up to her promise to cooperate with the Koehler family. She said that she would testify to the facts, regardless of whether it would help or hurt any party. Marie was apprehensive, but nevertheless was a credible witness. One aspect of Marie's testimony came as a complete surprise to Gushue. Marie was asked where she grew up, and she gave an address that was directly across the street from Gushue's house. Marie had moved out of her house the year before Gushue bought his home. Greg quickly assured Marie that he would not tell her parents about the depositions or the fact that she was a witness to the events of the senior week fatality.

After the depositions of Karen and Marie were concluded, Gushue scheduled the deposition of the manager of Ralph's Tavern. The questioning was low key and was concluded within a short period of time. The manager was not well prepared to deal with the deposition questions. It seemed as though he thought it would be a good defense if, in addition to lacking any memory of the senior week weekend, he demonstrated that the servers had little or no opportunity to observe their customers. He confirmed that the bar was very crowded on the night of the accident. It was unlikely that the bartender had the opportunity to talk to Jim. The bar was crowded two or three persons deep and people regularly ordered drinks from the very back of the crowd. Moreover, he said that the waitresses took orders from different groups of customers and that they could not be expected to know what each of their customers had been drinking. He said that he was not aware that Jim was under the influence of alcohol when he left the premises that night.

The testimony was just what Nancy Coolican was hoping for. Karen and Marie clearly established that Jim was a patron in Ralph's Tavern on the evening in question, the amount of alcohol that he had consumed beforehand, group purchases, and the switching of drinks from beer to schnapps. Nancy Coolican quickly used those facts to create a report that concluded that Ralph's Tavern was negligent and that its negligence was a proximate cause of the accident that occurred in Strathmere. Nancy's report was given to the attorney for Ralph's Tavern along with the other discovery responses.

Gushue had just returned to his office from a hearing in Pittsburgh when he saw a note on his desk that Angelo Martino had called. Angelo was a claims manager for Alistair Insurance Company. Greg and Angelo had just settled a major claim against the manufacturers of a bicycle and caliper brakes. The plaintiff in that case suffered quadriplegic injuries as a result of an accident. Greg represented the bicycle manufacturer and Angelo's company insured the manufacturer of the brake cable. Together, they settled the case for a reasonable amount that Angelo initially thought was too small. He was impressed by the way that Greg convinced a third defendant to participate in the settlement. When Greg saw the telephone note, he thought that there must have been some last minute problem with the settlement. He picked up the phone.

"Angie, Greg Gushue; I've got your note, what's going on? Is there a problem with the brake company?"

"No Greg, that one is over. I am calling you about a different case, the Koehlers and Ralph's. We insure Ralph's Tavern. I have just finished reviewing the file, including the report of Nancy Coolican. I want to know what the lowest amount that will settle this case is. If you give me a reasonable figure, I will try to get it for you."

It sounded straightforward but Greg knew what it meant. It was not an offer of settlement. It was a conditional response that Greg often used in dealing with his adversaries. You get someone to say what he will accept, and then you chisel him down to a lower number. The way that you normally handle that is to come back with a higher number that can be chiseled down to the number that you really want. However, the difference here was that Greg had a relationship with Angelo, and he did not want to lose that rapport.

In fact, Greg had given a lot of thought to the amount of an acceptable settlement. The death was instantaneous. Accordingly, the jury would award little or no damages for pain and suffering. The amount that the family could be expected to receive from Cindy over the remainder of her life was anybody's guess. A recent article in *The Philadelphia Daily News* reported the settlement of a wrongful death claim brought on behalf of a Cherry Hill, New Jersey high school student who died in a motor vehicle accident. The total amount of that settlement was $270,000. Fritz and Jeanne already received $300,000 from Jim's insurance company. The amount of a jury award on the claim against Ralph's would be speculative at best. Even if we win, we might lose, thought Greg. Gushue hesitated for a moment, and then responded, "Angie, I think that I can convince my clients to settle for $165,000." It was not an offer to settle the case for $165,000. It was a statement of opinion that Greg thought he could convince the clients to accept that amount, thus preserving the right to increase the amount if it was rejected by Alistair Insurance Company.

Within a week Angelo called and said that he was authorized to settle the case for the amount of $165,000. Fritz and Jeanne quickly agreed to the settlement. They were tired of the lawsuit and wanted to bring it to an end. The one-third legal fee for the dram shop part of the claim was $55,000. An annuity was purchased for $100,000 to provide approximately $800 per month in tax-free income. The balance of the settlement went to Fritz and Jeanne after reimbursement of the law firm's additional costs.

It took nearly three years to bring the legal proceedings to a close. It was not easy for Fritz and Jeanne, but they learned a lot. They had not been prepared to be thrown into this situation and they were well aware that much of it required professional expertise. They sought advice from every available source. The school and the church personnel were especially helpful. And when it came down to the wire, Fritz and Jeanne made every important decision themselves. In the meanwhile, their three other children required attention and guidance, and it was always there.

Cindy left us more than twenty years ago. About a dozen years back, Fritz passed away. They said at the funeral that he never recovered from Cindy's death. That may well have been the case. Cindy's brother and two sisters finished school with excellent academic records. It was not always easy for them. Now, they are well underway with their own lives. Jeanne knows better than anyone that she cannot live in the past. But she cannot help thinking about Cindy and what might have been. What would Notre Dame have held for her? And what after that? A graduate degree? And where? She thinks only of the positives.

Every week, Jeanne receives mail that reminds her of Cindy. Typical are the solicitations from State Street Financial Inc., seeking to buy Jeanne's remaining annuity payments. "Why wait?" They promise, "Cash now!" The inducements come in a variety of shapes and sizes. Some letters enclose facsimiles of bank checks made payable to Jeanne in amounts or $50,000 or more. In the lower right corner of the facsimile is a small-print note, "This is not a real check."

State Street and the others want Jeanne to sell them her remaining annuity payments for a price that they call "present value," a reduced amount that will be further reduced by attorneys' fees, court costs and possibly administrative charges assessed by the annuity manager. In the present tough economic times, it is a great deal for State Street, but less so for Jeanne. These are offers that she can – and does – refuse. Jeanne has not forgotten where the money came from, and why she and Fritz created the annuities.

How would Cindy have touched the future? The fact is that Cindy did touch the future; just not in the way that anyone expected.

Epilogue

"The past is prologue." It is a line from *The Tempest*, by Shakespeare. Also, it is inscribed on a monument outside the National Archives Building in Washington, D.C. Often you see it coupled with another line, as follows: "The past is prologue; the future is epilogue."

Bernard G. Segal, the chairman of our law firm, adopted that inscription as the firm's motto. Bernie explained the motto by telling a story of a tourist who, upon seeing the inscription outside the National Archives Building, asked the taxi driver, "What does it mean?" The cabbie responded, "Lady, that means '*You ain't seen nothing yet!*'"

I'll let it go at that.